ISAAC BRUCE

Acclaim for Isaac Bruce

"Isaac is devout in everything that he does. You never get only part of Isaac. When he commits to something you get his whole heart and soul. This starts first and foremost with his Christian beliefs and values and carries over to the way that he plays football. It is this passion teamed with God-given abilities that truly sets Isaac apart both on and off the football field. He is a man that I am honored to call my teammate and brother, not only on the field, but in the game of life."

—Kurt Warner
Quarterback, St. Louis Rams

"Isaac is much more than a great football player. His unusually high character and integrity causes him to stand out from the rest of us. He sets a standard on and off the field that is hard to match. He is simply special."

—Mike Martz
Head coach, St. Louis Rams

"Isaac wants us to know that what makes him important is not primarily that he caught the winning touchdown in the Super Bowl, or that he played in the Pro Bowl, or that he has the privilege to play a child's game for a living . . . rather, the wisdom of Isaac Bruce is that he clearly understands that it is 'God's love for him' that makes him important . . . and that truth should encourage us all."

—Kyle Rote Jr.
CEO, Athletic Resource Management
Author of *Beyond the Goal* and
Complete Book of Soccer

ISAAC BRUCE

Family, Faith, and the Final Touchdown

Jimmie Hand

PROVIDENCE HOUSE PUBLISHERS
Franklin, Tennessee

American Sports Heroes Series

04   03   02   01   00   1   2   3   4   5

Library of Congress Catalog Card Number: 00-103836

ISBN: 1-57736-200-4

Cover design by Gary Bozeman

Cover photos and photos on pages 102, 167, and 173 courtesy NFL Photos

Illustrations © 1999–2000 www.arttoday.com

PROVIDENCE HOUSE PUBLISHERS
238 Seaboard Lane • Franklin, Tennessee 37067
800-321-5692
www.providencehouse.com

To my wife of thirty-plus years, Freda,
and my wonderful children,
Debbie, Tami, Pamie, Susi, Christie, and Josh.
Thanks for putting up with an old man.
I love you all!

And I want to thank my brother Donnie
for always being there when I needed someone.
Thanks bud!

Wherefore seeing we also are compassed about with so great a cloud of witnesses, let us lay aside every weight, and the sin which doth so easily beset *us*, and let us run with patience the race that is set before us,

Looking unto Jesus the author and finisher of *our* faith.

—Hebrews 12:1–2a

ISAAC BRUCE

Contents

Preface   xi

Acknowledgments   xv

1. The Dream   3
2. The Early Years   11
3. Receive My Instruction   21
4. School Days   33
5. A Talk with Isaac's Mother   49
6. Getting to Know You   65
7. Waiting for the Draft   77
8. Getting Ready for 1999   85
9. A One-Game Winning Streak   95
10. Winning Ways Continue   107
11. America's Team?   115
12. The Second Half   123
13. Rams Clinch Playoff Berth   133
14. Home Field Advantage   141

15. Super Bowl Week   153
16. The Game   163
17. A Great Year!   171

American Sports Heroes Series   175
About the Author   176

Preface

WHEN I SAT DOWN WITH ISAAC BRUCE TO WRITE A BOOK ABOUT HIS YOUNG LIFE I WAS REMINDED OF MY EARLY childhood. Most Sunday afternoons when I was twelve or thirteen years old, I would jump out of bed (something that was not part of my character) and head west toward the Pacific Ocean which was a mere three blocks from my home in Redondo Beach, California. From there, I could catch the Red Car (an electric trolley) to go to downtown Los Angeles where things were happening! It has always amazed me that for ten cents you could ride so far and see so many different and wonderful things. Riding through the ethnic communities with their distinct and glorious smells made my taste buds go wild. Many of those foods that I got a whiff of my pallet would never have the opportunity to taste, but the wonderful aromas still linger as I think back.

In today's world it probably would not be prudent for a twelve-year-old boy to travel into downtown Los

Angeles all by himself, but this was a different time and a different world.

The Red Car arrived at the Los Angeles Coliseum at about 10:30 A.M. I'd then walk across the campus of the University of Southern California (USC) heading towards the Los Angeles County museum. Imagining that I was a member of the elite USC Trojan football team and running as a tailback up and down the field against archrival UCLA (University of California, Los Angeles), I tried to make my best moves just in case any Ram scouts were watching. In my dreams I was "Jaguar" Jon Arnett, the man with a thousand moves. Unstoppable, that was me!

The Los Angeles County Museum was one of my favorite places in the entire world. It had so many exhibits; it was like a big three-ring circus. I liked best the Old West exhibits with Buffalo Bill and Wild Bill Hickok, but the dinosaurs were right up there near the top on my all-time list. And still I had only spent ten cents. (I did buy a Baby Ruth candy bar before I got on the bus at Dad's Candy Store. That was a nickel.)

But now it was time to dig into my pocket and pay for what I had been thinking about all week—lunch at the museum cafeteria. I was sure that this had to be the finest restaurant on the planet. There was food of every kind from counter to counter. Many things there I had never seen or tasted, and most of them would remain untasted. For me it was always the meat loaf, mashed potatoes, green beans, and a small green salad (which I passed on). And the best part was that the meal was only twenty-five cents and came with a glass of milk and a piece of the best chocolate cake with the best chocolate icing that I have ever eaten.

After my wonderful lunch it was now time for the main event. The reason for my coming so far was the

Los Angeles Rams. The Rams were the darlings of the NFL (National Football League), playing their home football games in the L.A. Coliseum, and I was there to see them play the Baltimore Colts.

The Rams had only lost one game in the season with just three to go and looked to be a lock for the championship game against the Cleveland Browns. The Browns behind Otto Graham and Dante Lavelli were unbeaten and the Rams knew they had to win to keep pace with the fast charging San Francisco 49ers who were only two games behind them.

The price of my ticket was a whopping $2.50! It was not what most people thought of as a good seat, but to my way of thinking the higher up in the grandstand the better the seat. I'm not so sure that doesn't still hold up.

The Rams had two great quarterbacks, Bob Waterfield and Norm Van Brocklin. Along with the two quarterbacks came the usual Rams curse, a quarterback controversy. Their receivers were some of the best in the game. "Deacon" Dan Towler, their young divinity student, was a halfback with fullback size and speed and could catch the ball coming out of the backfield.

The receivers were led by Elroy "Crazy Legs" Hirsch. They called him Crazy Legs because when he ran his feet moved like propellers on an outboard motor. He was the long bomb "go to" man, Tom Fears was the possession receiver, and between the two of them they were nearly impossible to defend.

A lot has changed since those days. The Red Car has not run from Redondo Beach to Los Angeles for some time and if it did you wouldn't ride for ten cents. The museum is still there but I'm not sure if they are still serving that good-tasting meat loaf. It would probably be four dollars, and I am sure the price of a ticket at the coliseum has long since passed $2.50.

Many major changes have occurred. The Los Angeles Rams are now the St. Louis Rams. The Colts are now the Indianapolis Colts. I can't recall how that long ago game with the Colts came out, but I can tell you this—the St. Louis Rams are now World Champions after winning Super Bowl XXXIV.

Many things about the Rams remain just as wonderful as ever. Kurt Warner, an outstanding young Rams quarterback, had an MVP year that could only be found in a fiction novel. Marshall Faulk, an all purpose back, can catch with the best of them, and they have a young receiver corps headed by the sensational all-pro wide receiver Isaac Bruce who came back from a couple of injury-ridden seasons to be the "go to" man all year long.

Some things change and some things don't. . . .

Acknowledgments

I WOULD LIKE TO THANK THOSE MANY PEOPLE WHO HELPED MAKE THIS BOOK HAPPEN. WITHOUT THEM THERE WOULD BE NO ISAAC Bruce story. Thank you all!

First and foremost, I extend my thanks to Isaac Bruce for inspiring me to write this book. His is a wonderful example of a life lived by walking in faith. Also, many thanks to Karetha Bruce, Isaac's mother, for sharing her stories and photographs of the Bruce family history.

A special thank-you goes to Andrew Miller, Stephen James, and the staff of Providence House Publishers who orchestrated the publication of this material so skillfully.

Al Moak, my editor, deserves my gratitude for always making my words sound better (and he has the patience of Job). Bless you brother!

Thank-you to Paul Sheldon, my business partner, for relieving me of many of my duties so I had time to write.

I also extend my thanks to Ann Sheldon for doing a great job in transcribing tapes for me on short notice.

ISAAC BRUCE

The public relations staff of the St. Louis Rams supplied me with everything I ever wanted to know about the team, and I thank them.

My gratitude also goes to NFL Photos for supplying the pictures for our cover.

And last but not least, I want to thank the Marketing Arm, the sports agency that handles Isaac's personal affairs, especially Mark Clayton, Darin Perry, and Jeff Chown.

ISAAC BRUCE

CHAPTER ONE

The Dream

IT LOOKS LIKE THE CINDERELLA LOS ANGELES RAMS MAY HAVE REACHED THE END OF THE GLORY ROAD HERE ON A SNOWY JANUARY afternoon in Atlanta. Inside the Georgia Dome it's a nice seventy-two degrees but on the field it's really heating up! This is Super Bowl XXII. St. Louis is seventy-seven yards away from the Oilers goal line with only fifty-five seconds to go, and only one time out left. It doesn't look good for this wonder team that hasn't been in this position all season. Trailing by four points, they'll have to move the ball down the field in a hurry and score a touchdown to win the game. A field goal wouldn't help them here. This is Al Michaels telling you I have never seen a Super Bowl game with the excitement this game has shown. It has been exciting from the opening kickoff. We've had everything you could ask for in a championship game. I'm sure this will go down as the best Super Bowl ever played.

"Here we go, the Rams are huddling back on the fifteen-yard line. The quarterback seems to be looking at Isaac Bruce, the all-pro wide receiver as if to say, 'if we're going to do it, it's up to you!' Bruce just nods his head slightly. They come up to the line of scrimmage . . . the Oilers dig in . . . it seems as if everything is moving in slow motion . . . the quarterback has the ball, he's dropping straight back to pass, his offensive line is doing a great job of pass blocking, but his hope of getting the ball to number 80 doesn't look good because Bruce is double covered by a cornerback and a safety, but the quarterback lets it go. Wow! Wait a minute! . . . Bruce has the ball! . . . Isaac Bruce has made the impossible catch! I don't believe it! Number 80 made a circus catch between two Oiler defenders and now he has only one man to beat to get into the end zone and give the Rams their first ever Super Bowl victory. He turns left and heads toward the goal line. . . ."

"Isaac, Isaac its time to wake up son. You don't want to be late for your first day of junior high school do you?" asked Karetha Bruce as she smiled at her lanky son who was rubbing his eyes and trying to wake up.

"No Ma," he said stretching and yawning, "I won't be late. What's for breakfast? I'm hungry."

"My, young man, you should weigh two hundred pounds the way you eat," said his mother laughing. "How about some pancakes?"

"I'm Jimmie Hand and I'm sitting here with Isaac Bruce and I've got a question. Isaac, did you ever have a dream like that?"

"Sure I did, many, many times. I think every athlete has had that dream, if he didn't he wouldn't be much of a competitor in my books."

"I did a little figuring last night, and if you took one-half of the male population, that would be 150 million. And if only ten percent of those dreamed that dream, and we've had thirty-four Super Bowls, that's over a half million dreamers, and Isaac Bruce is the only one out of that half-million to have his dream come true. Those are pretty big odds! Don't you think?"

"I knew the odds were pretty big but I never quite looked at it like that. I know when you have God on your side, the odds, no matter how big, are in your favor. I knew if I went out there and did my job, God would do his, and He did."

"Isaac, there are a number of things I think we both would like to accomplish with this book. We want to let the readers know who the real Isaac Bruce is that made that dream catch as a player, as a person, as a man of God. But before we get into this I feel your fans would like to get inside Isaac Bruce for one play in a game, one game when he was catching the winning touchdown in the Super Bowl. With a billion people watching you.

"Would you walk us through the actual play from the time you went into the huddle until you crossed the goal line for a touchdown? When you went into the huddle you were seventy-seven yards away from a touchdown, there were fifty-five seconds left in the game, and you have only one time out left. Not a pretty picture. What was the atmosphere like in the huddle?"

"Actually Jimmie, we have to go back to the previous series. That's when the momentum shifted from us to the Titans and momentum means a great deal, especially in sports. On our last possession we had gone three-and-out, and we had to punt the ball. When they got it they moved right down the field and got a field goal, and the score was tied 16–16, and they could smell victory. You could see it in their eyes. But we weren't done yet.

"I kept telling myself, 'just keep repeating the prayers that you prayed about this game during the week.' I continued to believe: I confessed that I believed God when He said, 'it shall be as it was told unto me.' So I didn't get crazy about it. I didn't get overly anxious about it. I didn't get scared. My adrenaline was flowing, without a doubt, because I was in a football game. But I mean I didn't see any wide eyes in the huddle. Everyone was calm. We knew what we had to do. Just stay focused for another fifty-five seconds and play Rams football. But I'll tell you this, fifty-five seconds can be an eternity on the football field!"

"Whenever Kurt Warner called the play was it a play-action pass or was it a straight drop back from the get-go?"

"It was a drop back and I knew the ball was coming to me. As soon as I heard the play, I knew it was my ball!"

"Call the play for us?"

"It's called, twins right, H right, nine-ninety-nine, H below."

"Which of those designates you and what you're to do?"

"I'm H, doing a nine route, a streak."

"Okay, the play's been called, you're positive the ball will be coming to you. Now you come to the line of scrimmage. You are spread wide right. How was the cornerback playing you?"

"He came right up on me. They had been playing 'bump and run' most of the day. He was right there in my face. I expected more bump and run."

"Was there any trash talking going on?"

"You know what? The thing that's funny is we had played Tennessee previously, down in Nashville in a close game where they beat us. Both teams were very hyped. They were like 5 and 1 and we were 6 and 0. There was plenty of trash talking going on in that game. But once we got to the Super Bowl, I wouldn't allow myself to talk trash. I wanted to remain focused, and no matter what happened, I didn't want to go out and get into a jaw-jacking contest with someone else and get thrown off my job at hand. So there was a little from their part, but not very much. I knew I didn't want to get into it. I'm normally a guy who would probably say a couple of things, but this was the Super Bowl. This was maybe the biggest game I'd ever play in."

"What were some of the things the cornerback was saying to you?"

Isaac was smiling. "He was saying 'it's going to be a long day for you.' Now remember they would probably say it and structure it totally different than I'm giving it to you," he said laughing. "They would just say what you're not going to do to them, or what they're going to do to you or how long it's going to happen. It's strange, but I think cornerbacks talk more trash than any other position, but maybe it's because I see more of them. My friend in the NBA [National Basketball Association] tells me there's some real trash talking going on all the time out there."

"Here you are: you're up there ready to go and you're pretty sure the ball's going to come to you, right . . ."

"I'm almost 100 percent sure."

"So you're really sure?"

"Right. Take it to the bank. It's going to be mine."

"Are you nervous at all at that time?"

"No, not nervous. I stay level. If I don't stay level I could foul things up."

"The ball is snapped and Kurt Warner is dropping back to pass. He was getting great pass protection, how much trouble did you have getting by the corner?"

"Really, no problem at all because we had the same situation about three or four times earlier in the game and I had gotten off the line of scrimmage against him fairly well. I didn't expect anything different this time. So what happened was I kind of got off the line with no hesitation and just got upfield real quick. Since I had beaten him a couple of times, he wanted to try and stay on top of me, which is to get a kind of cut-off angle once the ball's in the air, so he could cut me off from the ball. We were running stride for stride, and he couldn't get the angle. Then I saw the ball leave Kurt's hand and, like I said, it was coming to me."

"In recalling the play, if I remember right it seemed like you were between two of the Titan defenders when you caught the ball. Was their strong safety coming over too?"

"Exactly. The safety follows Kurt's eyes. So wherever Kurt looks, he's going that way. So what happened is I'm running stride for stride with the guy and I'm running full speed. I never slowed down. I didn't give them any indication that the football was coming. Like I say, I was running stride for stride with the guy, I never slowed down. And once I saw the ball coming, I stopped and made the catch. Then the corner tried to reach back for the ball, but he was off balance and couldn't make the play and the guy running with me just fell, I'm not sure why but he just fell. Since the safety thought the ball was going to be over the top, he went over the top. I cut underneath him, kind of simultaneously as I caught the football."

"After getting by the two defenders you had just one guy to beat for the touchdown . . ."

"Yeah."

"What was it like when you looked down the field? Did it seem like you could just reach out and touch the goal line or did it seem like it was a mile away?"

"The goal line didn't seem that far away at all. I just knew I had to beat that last guy and I'd have the score."

"I've got to ask you this. I've talked to players in various sports who have played in big games when one big play has it all on the line. Some guys will tell me, 'When this all happened it seemed like slow motion.' Others say, 'it seemed like fast forward.' Or others just say, 'It seemed like a normal play, it just happened to be in the Super Bowl or the World Series. How did you see it?"

"Honestly, when it was happening, it just seemed like any other play. Now after, when I look at it on television, I didn't know that I used so much end zone. I thought I just barely got in by the pylon. But I have to tell you this, being in the Super Bowl did raise my concentration a bit."

"That had to be a great feeling crossing the goal line. Tell us how that felt."

"It was something. At first I didn't really feel it. But I can tell you I saw the fans. But I didn't hear anything. They were jumping up and down, hollering, and going wild, but I didn't hear a thing. I recently learned that in the end zone I knelt down after the touchdown and I didn't even remember doing that."

"We noticed that after you scored the touchdown and dropped the ball in the end zone, you ran out of the end zone toward the stands and raised your hands. Tell us about that."

"Oh yeah, oh yeah! I was thanking God for staying true to His Word as He always does. I can't express how I felt at that exact moment. It was super."

"Thank you very much for that Isaac. That may be as close as we readers ever get to catching the winning touchdown in the Super Bowl."

CHAPTER TWO

The Early Years

SOUTH FLORIDA WAS A GREAT PLACE TO GROW UP IN THE 1970S AND 1980S IF YOU WERE AN ELEVEN- OR TWELVE-YEAR-OLD BOY THAT kept his feet moving. It sure was ideal for young Isaac Bruce who was born in Ft. Lauderdale on just an average November eleventh evening in 1972 at 11:57 P.M. (all babies seem to be born in the middle of the night). He'll tell you it's his world, these white sandy beaches with the warm ocean waters, and the green parks with their tall, thin, swaying palm trees (always there to remind you that you're living in paradise). The athletic fields, Little League, youth football, basketball, and fishing all kept a young lad busy and out of trouble. Fishing had and still has a special place in Isaac's heart. What Florida boy doesn't like to fish? Isaac would fish for whatever was biting at the time.

In the freezing months of December and January, when boys up North were out shoveling snow and turning their attention to winter sports, the boys in South

Florida were still playing football in their shorts and sneakers. They would play around the clock. He and his friends could always find enough kids to get a game up even if they had to let Isaac's sisters play.

For Jesse and Karetha Bruce, children were a blessing from God, and they had truly been showered with blessings! Eight girls and seven boys made up this energetic brood, from the oldest, Verna, to Isaac's little brother Joseph. In between there are Theresa, Emanuel, Sylvia, Lucious, Charlotte, Shane, Willie, Samuel, Demetrius, Julianna, Christine, and Rosalind. All of the Bruce children have been raised by the Word of God and have stayed close to the Lord all these years.

When asked to describe his family Isaac said, "We weren't rich, that's for sure but we weren't poor either.

Isaac at six months.

12

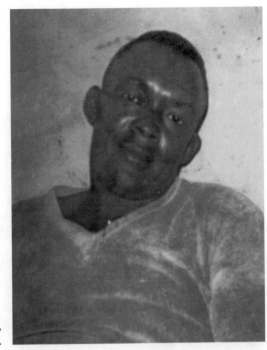

*Jesse Bruce,
Isaac's father.*

We seemed like all the other families of my friends. Oh, sometimes we had to sacrifice but most of the time we had everything we needed. It wasn't any big deal. It didn't take a lot of money to keep us happy. My mother taught us to share with others that were in need."

Jesse Bruce was born in Albany, Georgia, but moved down to Ft. Lauderdale to go into business. After working for years as a roofer he finally had his own roofing company. Roofing is a hot, backbreaking business, one that Isaac tried briefly a couple of times before he realized that getting a college education might be a better avenue for him. Anything looked better than dodging debris that the real roofers threw from up above while he was trying to pick up the trash and carry it to the nearby trucks to be hauled away. One funny thing

Top row: Shane holding baby Rosalind, Willie, and Lucious. Middle row: Demetrius and Samuel. Bottom row: Christine, Julianna, Isaac.

that Isaac relates about his short career as a roofer was that at home his father was called Dad but on the job he was Mr. Bruce. "That could get a little crazy at times," Isaac reported.

Karetha Bruce is a dedicated mother who believes and practices the Word of God in raising her children. "Ma raised us all the same, by the Word!" said Isaac, remembering back. "She even read the Bible to us while we were still in the womb." The Bible continues to be a big part of Isaac's life.

"She could be tough but she was gentle tough. If there was a problem or dispute, she would get the Bible out and say, 'sit down here and let's see what the Word

14

says about this.' And that was how things were settled in the Bruce household. She would say, 'That's not my word, it's God's Word.' And there was no arguing that."

Isaac was not allowed to hang out with a bad crowd. "My Ma really checked everyone out that came by the house to get me! But I was never drawn to the rowdy kids. I was a guy who just liked to hang with my friends. We'd go play basketball at the playground or the gym. We'd go to the Grand Prix and race go-carts, now that was fun. We played video games and that type of stuff but my mother always seemed to know where I was and what I was doing. It was almost spooky."

The large four-bedroom house that was home to all the Bruce children had a warmth about it that only a home filled with the Holy Spirit can have. There was a big kitchen where Isaac's mother fixed wonderful dinners, a large living room where the clan and their friends would

Isaac, age seven.

gather to talk, play games, or just rest up between adventures; it was a safe haven. The big grass yards both in the back and the front of the house had many touchdowns scored on them with neighborhood kids dreaming and trying to emulate their favorite players.

Isaac was no different. His dream was of playing for the Miami Dolphins. That was in the era of the Marks brothers, Mark Duper and Mark Clayton, but Isaac was always number 80, Nate Moore, when the games got underway. He could see himself catching the winning touchdown from Dan Marino. He never wanted to play any position other than receiver. He grew up watching great receivers like Lynn Swann, John Stallworth, and anyone he figured he could learn something from.

Left to right: Joseph, Rosalind, Elijah, and Isaac.

The Bruce family on Easter Sunday. Left to right, top row: Charlotte, Sylvia, Verna the pastor. Second row: Demetrius, Willie, Samuel. Third row: Julianna, Sara, Isaac, Christine. Fourth row: Rachel, Britt, Rosalind.

One thing that Mrs. Bruce would not allow was fighting and arguing. According to Isaac, "She could be a stern force to be dealt with if you got out of line." She taught her children there were better ways to settle problems than fighting. The book of Proverbs was one of her main road maps to good parenting.

Going to church was a way of life in the Bruce home. Sunday school, Sunday morning, and Sunday evening services, and mid-week service saw the entire Bruce family worshipping at Springs of Living Water, a Full Gospel church in Ft. Lauderdale, where Isaac was baptized when he was twelve years old by pastor Donahue.

Born and raised in Ft. Lauderdale, Karetha was a stay-at-home mom until all her children were grown and out on their own. With fifteen active kids, an outside job might have been a wonderful escape, but she was called to be the mother of "the blessings of God Almighty." Finally, and only after all of the at-home parenting, did she take a job at Isaac's old high school. Not that she is not still there for her children anytime they come calling. The children are constantly in touch with "Ma" when they need solid advice or just to talk. "Let's see what the Word says," is always "Ma's" first move.

Isaac came by his athletic ability honestly from a group of outstanding athletes in his family. His father, an ex-Marine, didn't play any organized sports but was a very athletic man. Playing with older, bigger, and stronger brothers and sisters made sports with the other neighborhood children easy for Isaac. Sister Charlotte was an outstanding softball player who went on to college at Albany State, in the town where their father was born and raised.

Isaac's brother Samuel was probably the most gifted athlete of the family until Isaac came along. Football was his favorite sport but "he was outstanding in any thing he tried," says Isaac. A quarterback in high school, Samuel was an all-around player.

Lucious was the first Bruce boy to play organized football, and he was an outstanding cornerback in high school. Lucious was not Isaac's oldest sibling but the one he most "looked up to." Lucious was exactly eleven years older than his little brother but everything he did, Isaac wanted to emulate. "He was a big influence on my life," says Isaac. "I remember when he got old enough he got a job. He got up and went to work everyday, and that impressed me. He had a nice car that I used to ride around in with him. We would take walks just to talk. I could talk about anything with Lucious. We'd talk about

Top row: Shane, Lucious, Willie, Demetrius, Samuel. Second row: Sylvia, Charlotte. Third row: Isaac, Christine, Julianna.

life. He was so easy to talk with, just like now. We can share anything!"

By the time that Isaac was growing into his preteen years it was pretty much he and his three sisters and Joseph that were still at home. The other siblings had grown up and left the nest but were always around to visit and offer help when needed.

Isaac's family isn't surprised by his success in football because they started to notice their brother was something special when he got into high school. They had followed him through Little League and all the other youth sports. However, when he started to play serious football at Dillard High School, his God given talents were starting to come forward, even though it took a while for him to reach the level of success that he has achieved.

"When success came to me I think my family thought mostly that the blessings of God had been bestowed upon me and I hoped I could help my family financially and become a good testimony to the Lord." This was the thinking of a young athlete, a real role model, who never actually made the starting team until his final year at Memphis State University.

Receive My Instruction

ISAAC, I KNOW YOU'VE BEEN A CHRISTIAN ALL OF YOUR LIFE. LET'S TALK ABOUT SOMETHING THAT I KNOW IS DEAR TO YOUR HEART, THE Lord Jesus Christ."

"Right on, you know that's my favorite thing to talk about. There is nothing bigger in my life than my relationship with Almighty God. Nothing!"

"Not even football?"

Laughing, "I like football very much and it's been good to me, but its way down the ladder in importance. As I said, Jesus is my Savior and best friend. My parents and my brothers, sisters, and friends have been and will be with me when my football days are over. I just thank God for all He's done in my life. I promise you this—He will never fail you."

"We know you started to attend church as an infant at Springs of Living Water in Florida, but can you remember how old you were when you were truly born again?"

"I'm not exactly sure, I was pretty young, maybe eight or nine. Brother Wayne Donahue led me to the Lord and I was baptized when I was around twelve but I was around it all my life."

"Tell us a little bit about how your parents made the Word mean so much to you and your brothers and sisters."

Chuckling, "I'm sure you can tell by now that my mom is very special to me. I could talk about her all day. In our home we had devotions every morning and while we were getting ready for school, Ma was walking the halls reading the Bible to us. She made it a point of getting it into us at every chance. We would get up early every morning, even Saturdays, to hear the Word."

"Did you ever resent all that, getting up early?"

"I never resented the Word. . . . Oh, I probably resented sometimes getting up so early in the morning on Saturdays, considering that I got up early every morning to go to school, but I'm positive that in the long run it helped me tremendously. I'm sure glad she made me do it!"

"How do you find time to spend time in the Word with your busy schedule?"

"The Word of God in Matthew, says 'seek ye first the kingdom of God and his righteousness and all things will be added unto you,' so I try to get up early in the morning and let that be the first thing I do before I do anything else."

"Has the Bible always been such an important part of your life as it is now?"

"Oh yes. Without a doubt. I mean it is important. I believe that it's not only important to feed the body but to feed the spirit as well. I think reading the Word, or listening to the Word on tape, or reading books that emphasize the Word, feeds the spirit.

"There are going to be many battles in your life, sometimes little ones, sometimes big ones, and anytime that there's a spiritual battle, you'd best know what your spiritual weapons are. The Word lets you know what they are and how and when to use them. The Word is a spiritual weapon. The name of Jesus is a spiritual weapon! And we have to remember that.

"With this world seemingly going to hell in a hurry it's very hard for young people to stay on the right track. Peer pressure, lack of real home life, no rules to guide or set a course with, and add to all that the problems created by drugs, alcohol, and illicit sex, and it makes it real hard for kids today."

"Speaking of the name of Jesus being a spiritual weapon, I understand from an article I read in the *St. Louis Post Dispatch* that you recently had firsthand knowledge of just how powerful that Name is when you were involved in a near tragic car accident. Can you fill us in on that?"

"It's true and I can tell you firsthand just how powerful that Name is! I was driving eastbound on highway 70 when the rear left tire blew out. I was heading for a gully, about to roll over driver side first. The Mercedes flipped twice before landing upright. All at once my mother's teaching came to my mind and I let go of the steering wheel and threw up my hands and shouted 'Jesus' for protection."

"That had to be a scary situation. Were you afraid of dying as the car continued to roll?"

"No! I knew what the outcome would be once I spoke the name of Jesus. Once I got that out of my mouth, I wasn't afraid. I knew I was covered by the blood of Jesus. I found out later that something else happened on

The Mercedes that flipped during Isaac's accident.

Sunday when Bishop Patterson at my home church in Memphis felt led to pray for me."

Patterson said, "I didn't have a premonition of Isaac's accident. I want to make that clear. But we were having our 8 A.M. communion service and asking for prayers. And suddenly, I said to the congregation, 'The Lord has placed in my spirit to ask you to pray for Brother Isaac Bruce. So we ask the Lord to bless him, protect him, be with him.' The people thought it was strange that I would mention Isaac at that time. But the Lord just dropped it into my spirit. God saw what was coming."

"Isaac, I understand your mother had a similar experience years before. Is that true?"

"Yes. She was driving from New York to Florida with the station wagon filled with her kids when she also blew

Left: Isaac's brother Samuel with his wife, Tracy.

Below: Isaac's niece Elaine, daughter of his sister Shane.

Bottom: Samuel, Isaac's brother

their shoulders. What kids learn from the Word of God, once they become believers, and if they've received the Holy Spirit, it'll check them. I don't think they'll be doing some of the things that are so prevalent in this world. The Bible is the best parenting manual out there. I know it worked for my mom."

"I know that most of the teams around the NFL have Chaplain Programs or Bible studies for the players. Do the Rams have anything where other Christians get to together and share the Word of God?"

"Oh yeah. We have a weekly Bible study. We've had the Bible studies ever since I've been affiliated with the team. I know it helps to be in the Word with other believers who face the same kinds of problems that you as a professional athlete face. You can help each other through the rough spots, encourage one another when things aren't going just right, and we all have trials."

"Who are some of the other Christians on your team?"

"Kurt Warner, Ray Agnew, Ernie Conwell, D'Marco Farr, Kevin Carter. . . . I've probably forgotten to mention some . . . there's a bunch of guys."

"It is important to bear one another's burdens and have someone to talk to that is a believer and can feel where you are coming from. I remember a few years ago, Charles Mann, the great defensive end from the Washington Redskins, told me that they used to have Monday morning prayer groups where Christians would come and share their problems of the past week. Charles said that the main reason he didn't want to do anything wrong was he didn't want to face Art Monk. He said it was easier to face the Lord than Monk!"

"Right. It is good to have a brother that you are accountable to. I think young people, high school or college-age kids, would be well served if they could find someone their own age that they could be open with about their life and their life with the Lord. Sometimes just having someone to talk to can make a big problem look not so big."

"You have a home in Memphis. Where is your home church while you are there?"

"My home church in Memphis is Temple of Deliverance Cathedral of Bountiful Blessings. It's a Church of God in Christ—COGIC. It's a great church that I really enjoy."

"How do you handle church attendance when you are in St. Louis and with the Rams playing almost every Sunday?"

"It does create a problem unless we have a Saturday game or something like that, but I do attend whenever I can. I make sure I go to a Bible study at Family Christian Center in St. Louis during the week."

"In the newspaper and in other media, especially during Super Bowl week, it was mentioned that you are planning on going into the ministry when you finish playing football. Is that still an option?"

"It is," he answers hesitantly. "I like to say it like this . . . With what I'm doing now, football is the stage that God has given me, I'm sharing His Word every chance I get. I'm sharing the Gospel with others by continuing to give my testimony. So in a way, I'm already in the ministry. Only God knows where he'll use me in the future, but I just want to be ready when he calls."

"You're right about where you are today. Yours would be a hard witness to duplicate, Super Bowl champ, all-pro, and all the national attention you receive. Isaac, we all know the Christian life is not a happiness license where everything we do comes up roses from the moment we accept the Lord and Savior. I'm sure in your life you've had some real struggles. Can you talk about those tough times and how you got through them?"

"That's true. I wouldn't trade the Christian walk with anyone but it is not all a bed of roses. Sometimes it seems you no sooner accept Christ and the devil swoops down on you with every demon in hell."

"You're right about that. It's easy to praise God when you've just won the Super Bowl and made the all-pro team but what about those couple of years that were one nagging injury after the other?"

"Well, I tell you what: I didn't blame God for my hamstring injuries, because if anyone was missing it, it was me, because I know God can't fail. And you know, I think one of the big things that I didn't do was make myself stop running, like when I thought our practices were too long, and I thought we may have been out there too long, I didn't know how to stop myself. And there were no coaches around who would know and come up and say, 'Isaac, stop now, let someone else do this.' We didn't have those types of coaches. We probably didn't have them in the first three years of my being with the Rams. Fortunately we now have the kind of coaches that are in tune with my needs as a player.

"And I think another thing was I wasn't paying my tithes the way that I should have been, which was blocking my healing, because I knew the Word, and I needed to obey. I knew how to stand on the Word, but that was knocking it. It's what was counteracting my prayers. It was me not being faithful with my tithes."

"You know, so many people are that way, and I think we all go through it in our Christian life. And sometimes it takes something from God to get our attention, and it's amazing how, in talking to people on all income levels, it seems those people with the least have an easier time of tithing, for whatever reason, than those that the Lord has truly shown He is faithful. So you make a very good point."

"Right. God says He will open the windows of Heaven and shower us with blessings, but He warns us not to steal His tithes and offerings. And it is an easy trap to get yourself into. It's either He's God of all or not God at all."

"When you would pray, during those times when things were rough, how would you approach the Lord?

Pausing, "I wasn't angry. I didn't allow myself to get frustrated. I didn't get frustrated with football or with the hamstring injuries. I just didn't allow myself to, because, number one, I knew what type of player I was—I knew what I could do on the football field. It just so happened I had a pulled hamstring and couldn't run."

"Yes, you could have been a roofer and pulled a hamstring."

"Right. My dad had done it before so I knew it was something I needed in my life and worked through it. I continued to praise Him and ask for strength to get through this trial. I knew and believed He would get me through it as he has always done."

"Your degree from Memphis will be in education. Have you thought about teaching school when your playing days are over?"

"I thought a bit about substitute teaching about two years ago, once the season was over. I decided against it because I didn't want it to affect my training program and preparing to do what I get paid for. But it's still a possibility. I think I would enjoy it very much, and I think I could get over to the kids."

"I'm sure you could, once you got over the atmosphere of, 'Mr. Bruce is our teacher!' How long until you graduate?"

"I have just fifteen hours left. I'm close, real close."

"Do you have any advice you might share with the kids out there reading this and wondering if all this school stuff is really worthwhile?"

"The biggest thing would be—this is what I tell my little brother Joseph—make sure you get a degree. Focus on getting your high school and college diplomas, whether you're going to be a professional athlete or not. I look at it like this—in a positive way—I was going to be a professional athlete, but I wanted to get as close as I could to that degree, to be able to go back one summer and knock it out and get it off my mind. I think the biggest thing that we as athletes had was receiving scholarships—having someone else pay for your schooling and taking advantage of it.

"I don't believe that we took as much advantage of it as we should have. I know there were a lot of non-athletes out there who probably couldn't afford to go to school, but would have loved to be in the position we were in. So I let Joseph know every chance I get, that he should do well in school and prepare for the future whatever God brings his way, and that he should remember that there are a lot of great athletes out there who could have played professional sports but didn't have the grades to get into a college program where they could have been recognized as pro material."

CHAPTER FOUR

School Days

S ABLE PALM SCHOOL, NOW MARTIN LUTHER KING JR. ELEMENTARY WAS WHERE YOUNG ISAAC GOT HIS FIRST TASTE OF ORGANIZED tackle football. As you might expect he was one of those boys that was always chosen first when pickup games were being formed, and his raw but real athletic ability was already coming out. He could do running complete back flips like the Green Bay Packers by age eleven; he could jump higher that most of the kids his age, and he'd run everywhere he went, much like Forrest Gump.

Murder ball was the all-time favorite playground game for he and his friends, at least those with a strong heart and fast of foot. When asked to describe murder ball he smiled and said, "Murder ball is where you take whatever you can find to use as a ball. Maybe a tennis ball, or a wad of paper balled up or whatever else might be handy to make a ball. You toss it up in the air with a bunch of guys, maybe fifteen or twenty; there was no set number, everyone could give a try at murder ball. Then

Isaac, eight years old.

whoever touches the ball first has to score before he's tackled, and everyone is after him to bring him down! You know, murder him. It's one of those type games—a little made up as you go along. I'd play, get my clothes dirty before school started, and just go through the day.

"My Ma wouldn't be too thrilled about that, but she never caught me. Hey wait a minute here; did I just give myself up? Hey Ma what you just read was fiction."

Isaac went on to Dillard High School where he had the opportunity to play with some great high school athletes on the Panther championship team. Otis Gray was his first high school coach. "Coach Gray was a great motivator. He had the knack of bringing out the best in his players," Isaac recalled.

Right: Isaac's football career began at an early age.

Following page: One of Isaac's first team photos. He is in the top row, wearing number thirty-one.

34

Bruce Bush was Isaac's receiver coach in high school and was instrumental in his early development. "He taught me to catch the ball with my hands, that's one of the things he really emphasized about being a receiver. And route running . . . I ran routes 'til I could do them blindfolded. I am thankful to Coach Bush for that early start and all that he taught me that has helped me with the Rams."

The Panthers had a great team that went on to win the 4A Florida State High School Championship in 1989, Isaac's senior year. After a season that saw him lead his team in receptions he was named to the second team all-county. Not bad for a player who had not yet made the starting lineup.

When looking back with fond memories Isaac says, "I played with a group of guys at Dillard who were tremendously big and athletic for their ages. We were a team with a lot of players—I mean we never had fewer than ninety very talented players on the team. It was a tight school, where you had to wait your turn to play because everyone was that good. I was a guy who had to wait 'til I was a senior to play, like many others."

Dillard won the Florida 4A title in Isaac's freshman year in 1986 and again in 1989. In 1986 Isaac was still a long way from high school glory on the football field, but in 1989 he was one of the reasons the Panthers won again.

That team produced a number of outstanding athletes. Seven of them went on to play football at Division 1 schools. James Bostic, a running back, went on to Auburn University where he had an outstanding collegiate career and was drafted by the then Los Angeles Rams in the same draft that saw Isaac go in the second

Isaac, his little brother Joseph, and a friend on ring day at St. Thomas High School.

round, also to the Rams. Today there are still two players from that championship team playing in the NFL: another wide receiver, Frank Sanders of the Arizona Cardinals and Isaac Bruce. "Frank and I grew up together. We played Little League and all the other sports. He'll tell you today that I taught him everything he knows about being a receiver," says Isaac laughing.

Isaac's hope was to attend Purdue University in Lafayette, Indiana, in the fall on a football scholarship following his senior year. He had signed a national letter of intent with the Boilermakers, but when the time came to enroll he didn't have the grades, and his test scores were not high enough to get in. But he wasn't one to let things get him down. When asked if that rejection hurt his pride he answered, "I'd say I was only down for about half a day, really, because I looked at Purdue this way, it was going to be a big step and a big move for me, considering I was only seventeen years old. The possibility of going up north to Indiana, where it was going to be very cold with ice and snow, wasn't something I really was used to. But I had picked the school because I thought I could handle it. Had I gotten in, I'm sure I would have done all right.

"But for me to go to junior college, and go to Los Angeles, and meet the people that I met—it made me grow up a whole lot faster than I believe I would have at Purdue, because I wasn't on scholarship. I ended up having to pay my own bills, like rent, and pay for a phone, and making sure I kept it turned on so I could have communications with my family, so I grew up in a hurry."

Isaac and a friend during his college years.

Isaac was never one to let the grass grow under his feet even when he wasn't burning past an NFL corner-back. He was quick to rebound from the Purdue situation. Fortunately, a football coach from Purdue, Coach Dan Lowensberry, had a friend at a junior college in Southern California and recommended that they take a careful look at this young wide receiver from Florida with blazing speed.

West Los Angeles College (WLAC) is situated right in downtown Los Angeles. Isaac attended there for only one semester after arriving in California. Even though he was falling in love with southern California, with weather much like Florida's, he was becoming disenchanted with the football program at West Los Angeles. "Those guys would hit you! I mean hit!" There was some real talent on that team, but because they ran the triple option and Isaac wasn't an option type receiver ("I was big on catching, not real big on blocking"), he knew for his own career's sake he had to find a school that put the ball up in the air. Keyshawn Johnson was another receiver on the WLAC team and he went on to an outstanding career at USC and then with the New York Jets where he's one of the top players in the NFL. Keyshawn and Isaac have sort of gone their separate ways over the years. They only see each other when the Rams meet the Jets. "But, you know, West L.A. really wasn't bad for a local guy. If you lived in the area it was a fine place to go to school," says Isaac.

Just by chance Coach "Rock" Richmond was at WLAC one day watching the squad practice. He was a student at WLAC and coached at nearby Santa Monica Junior College (SMJC). Isaac and Coach Richmond got to talking and before he knew what hit him Isaac was visiting a practice at Santa Monica. Right then and there he knew this was the kind of team he wanted to be part of. He made the transfer at the semester break.

But at first it was a bit of an uphill battle. Isaac remembers a funny story about that: "I was in line preparing to run my first route at Santa Monica, and the receiver coach pulled me out and asked, 'Son, who are you?' I told him my name, told him my story, but he kind of brushed me off, and said, 'Well, whatever . . . get back in line and just do whatever.'

"By the time I got up and ran my first route . . . I told Rock about what happened. I said, 'Look, I don't think he wants me over here.' He said, 'don't let it bother you. Just go run your route and I promise you he's going to love you.' I said, 'Okay.' So I ran the route, and I didn't think I did anything special, I just ran the route the way I was taught to run routes, and I caught the ball the way I was taught to catch the ball. After he saw that catch, he was ready to be my best friend forever. To this day my coach and I are still close friends."

It was at Santa Monica that Isaac begin to notice his own skill levels and his ability to play football. Actually, he was able to play receiver much better than the other receivers he was seeing. Since he was a youngster, this was the first time he thought he could reach his dream.

Not really knowing any one in Santa Monica didn't seem to bother Isaac, as he was a person that didn't need a group of people around him to make him happy. Staying in touch by telephone with his family, he enjoyed his time in Santa Monica and has many fond memories of places and people.

There were some other perks that made this college stay a little easier. SMJC had the ability to help some of

*Isaac and a
college friend.*

the out-of-town players earn money to pay their rent. West L.A. hadn't been in a position to help their student athletes financially. With his mother's help, who was working to help him eat properly ("no hamburgers" she would say to her hungry son), Santa Monica made many things possible for Isaac that he might not have received somewhere else.

He played on outstanding teams in one of the premiere junior college conferences in the country, a conference that always produced top quality Division 1 athletes. The Corsairs were 9–2 in his second year there. Still not a starter, he made first team all-conference, leading the league in pass receiving.

He didn't have a problem about not making the starting team even though he was the team's leading receiver in both yards gained and touchdowns scored.

He understood that some of those guys had been around longer than him. Just the opportunity to play and excel was all he wanted.

From that Santa Monica receiver corps, one went to San Jose State University on scholarship and the other to Utah. But Isaac was the only member of that group to go on and make it in professional football.

At Santa Monica JC, he continued to have excellent coaches as he had in high school. Randy Fieder, his receiver's coach, helped him adjust to a new place and a new football program, which he was grateful for. He was able to handle it with ease.

After reviewing offers from Washington State, Cincinnati, Arizona, Colorado State, and several other schools, along with Memphis State University, it was Memphis that got the nod. When asked why he choose the Tigers he said, "Now it's my personal belief that there is no better football than in the South, and I wanted to play in the Southeastern Conference, the SEC, but no one really recruited me from there. But Memphis State had a couple of SEC schools on their schedule, so I signed with Memphis. Maybe to show the others what they missed."

During Isaac's two-year stay at Memphis, the Tigers had great talent but just couldn't put it all together on a regular basis. They were 6–5 both years. Isaac had no trouble adjusting to Division 1 football from junior college. Again he did not make the starting lineup right away but still led the team in receptions and touchdown catches.

When asked to talk about the big games with the SEC teams he said with pride, "We played Mississippi State my senior year down in Starkville, and, amazingly we won that game. That game was a real shootout. Balls were flying everywhere. We won 45–35.

"Another big game was in my junior year when we played Tennessee. We were 0 and 14 versus Tennessee lifetime. But this was a game we could have won, should have won. It was a close game going into the fourth quarter with about three minutes left. We made them punt, and the score was 23–21 in their favor. Now they were punting from their own end zone. It was for sure we'd get pretty good field position. We knew when we got the ball back we had a kicker who had won the Lou Groza award that year as the nation's leading field goal kicker. All we needed to do was field the punt, run a couple of plays, and kick the winning field goal and we would win 24–23. Not to be. Not to be the day that we broke the losing streak to Tennessee. Our punt return guy fumbled the ball, and they recovered it.

"During my time at Memphis, we'd have something called the TTP which was Typical Tiger Play; that was where something would go wrong if it was possible for it to go wrong and it always seemed to do that. Sort of like Murphy's Law.

"It was as though we played to everyone's level. We'd play to Tennessee's level. We'd play Mississippi State and play to their level, and then we'd play a team like Southwest Louisiana and play to their level and get beat! We were never able to get over that hill and put it together and play the good solid football that we were capable of."

Memphis was no different than the other places Isaac played. It didn't seem like much of a step up from junior college football for him. Even though he didn't get the starting role right away that you would expect for the top receiver for the Tigers, he realized there were returning receivers with talent and experience. He would wait his turn.

When asked how things started off at Memphis he recalled, "I remember my first day in pads. There were a number of incumbent receivers there when I got there. There was a lot of hype about us, a couple of junior college transfers, coming from southern California. When we were out on the field we'd see guys watching us, probably from the hill, who probably played the same position as us, and word was going out that we were making pretty good strides, that we were players.

"Coach Fieder, my position coach who had recruited me from Santa Monica, was planning on starting me probably at least half the season, but early on in practice we made a couple of plays during blitz drills, and I don't think anyone had been able to make those plays before I got there. It only took me about three days to become a starter. I started for the rest of my career at Memphis."

The big difference from junior college and Division 1 was speed. The whole of the team was fast. The linebackers were running a little faster. The defensive linemen were faster. Isaac was like good cream; he was always able to come to the top. Even though he was unable to lead the Tigers to a bowl game, he did give them many things to remember him by.

Now he divides his time between St. Louis and Memphis, but calls Memphis home. "I really don't have many friends in St. Louis, outside of football. The friends I have in Memphis are those I met when I was in college there and we began hanging out or whatever. These friends went through my struggles with me. They're

Isaac Bruce's personal friends, not Isaac Bruce the football player's friends."

When asked where he plans to settle down when his playing days are over he replied, "Florida without a doubt. I like that warm weather and the white sandy beaches. Yeah, I'll take Florida."

CHAPTER FIVE

A Talk with Isaac's Mother

BEFORE WE CONTINUE ON ABOUT RAMS-STYLE FOOTBALL, I WOULD LIKE TO TAKE A BREAK AND ASK YOU SOME QUESTIONS AND find out about the real Isaac Bruce. They're questions that I feel the readers would like to ask. I can think of no better person to start with than Isaac's mother Karetha.

"I'm sitting here speaking with Karetha Bruce to get some insight that only a mother could give on her favorite football player. First, let me compliment you on your son. I've been around ballplayers for over thirty years and I've never met anyone quite like Isaac. No only is he a great football player, he's a good kid!"

"I'm glad to hear you say that. I always enjoy hearing good reports about my children. I don't know what mother doesn't."

"What kind of child was Isaac?"

"When he was young he was a lot like he is now, quiet and mellow. I never had any problems with him. He always minded his momma. He was a very healthy baby

Isaac and Karetha Bruce clown for the camera.

from the time we brought him home from Holy Cross
Hospital here in Ft. Lauderdale. Really he was born in
Pompano, a suburb of Ft. Lauderdale that's just a few
miles up the road."

"You have raised fifteen children. Was that a terribly
hard job?"

"What a lot of people don't understand is that I had
my children in sets. I had one set and stopped for a while.
Then I had another set and stopped again for a while.
Then I had the last set. Now the last set consists of Isaac,
Rosalind, and Joseph. Isaac is three years older than
Rosalind, and Rosalind is six years older than Joseph. So
when Isaac came along some of the older kids were
grown and out on their own. All fifteen of them were

Karetha Bruce was six months pregnant with Isaac when this photo was taken.

never living in the house at the same time."

"How long have you and Mr. Bruce been married?"

"Forty-one years," she said with a smile in her voice. "Sometimes it seems like a long time and other times it seems like just yesterday that I got married."

"Did Isaac get along with his father?"

"Yes, he got along well with his father, but when he was very small, I won't say he and his daddy did not get along, but he didn't like his daddy too much at that time. He was a momma's boy and I know how that can be. I have got some girls that are daddy's girls. It's not that we don't get along, but when it comes down to solving a problem, it's their daddy first and I'm second. With the boys I'm first and Jesse is second. I don't know why that is but I've talked to other mothers who say the same thing. And I think it makes a difference if the mother is nursing, you know . . . did you ever come around a mother dog when they had a litter of puppies? They won't let you get near them! I think it's the same with kids."

"Did the older children help you with the younger children?"

"Well, they were helpful, but when it came down to my babies, I didn't allow my older kids to bother them. I tended the babies myself, because I didn't want them dropped or hurt. I was always a very concerned person when it came to my kids, especially my babies.

"When Joseph came along, it was a pleasure for them to hold and cuddle him because I didn't let the rest of

Isaac and Rosalind at a church picnic. Isaac was ten years old when this was taken.

Pastor Verna, Isaac's sister, with her children.

them do it earlier. I was the type of mother that wouldn't let people keep my children either!"

"Which of your children have the zeal for God that Isaac has?"

"My oldest daughter, Verna, has been pastoring at New Beginnings Church here in Ft. Lauderdale. She's married to Michael DuPont who also is a pastor at New Beginnings. Sylvia . . . now Sylvia is the third oldest daughter. I sent her to Rama Bible College in Tulsa, Oklahoma. She was there for four years and then started out ministering a little bit . . . then kind of got away from it but she's getting back into it now. And then you take Charlotte, she's finding her place in the ministry also."

"Did you find much difference in raising girls as opposed to boys?"

"I don't see any difference. Some people say that there is a big difference but I don't see any difference, because everybody's different. Take my oldest daughter . . . when she turned fourteen, she kind of rebelled. We have something here called Junior Haven, it's a place for youngsters to get help in straightening out their lives. After she was there awhile we moved her to Okella Christian school and by the time she was seventeen she had mellowed down.

"And my oldest son, he rebelled when he was sixteen. And so I don't see any difference, because girls or boys will both rebel when the enemy comes in. People always told me, say, from thirteen up 'til sixteen or seventeen are kind of bad years for teenagers, especially in today's world."

"Isaac was seventeen years old when he left for Los Angeles to go to college at West L.A. Junior College. Did you worry about him being out on his own so far from home for the first time?"

"No, I never was a worrier. I didn't worry about him . . . being seventeen years old. He first went to West L.A. for a year and then he met Coach Burrell in Los Angeles, and he got Isaac in Santa Monica Junior College for his second year.

"But I'm gonna tell you, the only thing that really vexed me with him. At that time our business was kind of shutting down, and I had a job of my own, and when he would call me, I would ask him, 'What have you eaten today?' And every time he said 'hamburgers.' That would hit my heart! That would bother me so, and I'm scraping

Verna DuPont poses with her mother, Karetha Bruce, after church.

money, sending it to him, you know, so he could eat. We were going through a few small bad spots in our business because during the rainy season the roofing business is not too good. . . . Even when people have leaks in their houses its hard to get out there and fix them.

"And so I had a job working at Dillard High School, the same school where Isaac graduated. As a matter of fact I went to school at Dillard, too. I also had another job out west of town . . . I would go out to this little Jewish woman's home and mostly keep her company, because she was there alone. I did whatever it took to keep his stomach full, because I couldn't stand hearing that he ate hamburgers!"

"Was dinner time a big deal in the Bruce household?"

Isaac came home from college to take his sister Rosalind to the prom.

Joseph, Isaac's little brother, and his mother at Joseph's contract signing with Missouri State University.

"Yes, I can tell you we didn't have hamburgers. Isaac wasn't much for vegetables though. The closest he wanted to get to a vegetable was corn. I told him if it isn't green it isn't a vegetable. Now soul food, chicken, rice, and gravy were his favorite foods."

"He says you are by far the best cook in the world."

"I don't know about that, but I do like to cook. We would have our dinner at the dining room table as a family. I always tried to cook good healthy meals and I didn't get any complaints."

"What advice did you give him when he left home?"

"Well, he always kept to himself, but I told him to pick his friends carefully, that running with a crowd wasn't good. I said be careful about the people you select. Stick with productive people, and people who are in church that want to do something for themselves and others. In this day and time it's kind of dangerous out there. Trust the Lord to guide your path. The Lord warns us to 'not be unevenly yoked' with one another."

"Did Isaac have a big appetite growing up?"

"Very good, very good! But I have a brother that lives in Elmira, New York, . . . he got a newspaper that had a story right after the Super Bowl. It said that Isaac learned to run so well because he has so many sisters and brothers, so he had to race them to the table. I'll tell you, that kind of annoyed me because that just wasn't true. You know, we were businesspeople . . . we had our own roofing company and we not only had all that we needed, we had plenty to give to other people."

"When I asked Isaac where he got his favorite dishes in St. Louis, he told me he only got them when his 'Ma' came to visit."

"Yes, when I come to St. Louis I always cook, and cook enough to freeze so when I'm not there he still gets momma's cooking. I told you he's not a vegetable person but when I'm there I make him eat vegetables."

"Do you remember the first time you saw your son play professional football with the Rams?"

"Yes I do. They were in Los Angeles at the time. They were the Los Angeles Rams, and I thought it was amazing . . . you know, like sometimes back in your Christian walk, you read in your Bible, or sometimes someone will come and give you a word of knowledge about promises that God had given you?" But somehow, you really couldn't touch that. You know, you just know what He said in His Word, and you just go along and hear what is said. But when I saw this, I began to see it coming to his face and I was amazed . . . I was really amazed. But I knew within myself that God had put us there, because there were promises that He had made me a long time ago before Isaac was ever born, He said if I'd walk upright before Him that He would bless me . . . I would be amazed.

"During my prayer time, sometimes the Lord would speak this to my spirit, but I had no idea of what He was talking about. But I went on in the fear of the light, and then I began to see it unfold when Isaac went pro. I am truly amazed at the ministry that God has given Isaac. The Lord has blessed him and me in so many ways."

"How do you feel about football?"

"Well . . . it's okay. I don't like all the physicalness of the game. They get knocked about too much, and I know in the years to come, except if the Lord gives Isaac a miracle, it may bother him some. Football is okay, but sometimes it's the guys that play football that kind of turn me off a little bit because they are so arrogant. I guess that's because so many people look up to them. But I like football. And this year I watched more games than I ever watched. I'm the one that carried my kids to Little League and other sports that they played. I get a little excited when I see him play now, but I'm not a hollering, screaming person."

"I'd like to ask you just a couple more questions. I'm sure you are proud of Isaac as he is of you, but if you could help young couples starting out today in marriage, and starting a family, what tips would you give them?"

"The first tip I would give them: to accept the Lord Jesus Christ as their savior. The Bible says without God we can do nothing. And, you can't even start out to raise a family or have a marriage without the Lord in it. Without the Lord it is also a strain on the children too. One parent is pulling this way, and the other is pulling that way. This makes your family divided.

Top: Karetha Bruce pins a deputy badge on Isaac's sister Sylvia.

Bottom left: Sara, Isaac's oldest niece.

Bottom right: Rachel DuPont, Isaac's niece and daughter of Verna.

Top: Shane, Isaac's sister, in a volleyball picture.

Middle: Isaac's brother Samuel

Bottom: Charlotte, another sister of Isaac's, in a volleyball picture.

"The second tip I would like to give, something I taught my kids: When you decide that you want to get married, seek God for a companion first. Go to Genesis, the twenty-fourth chapter and read what Abraham said to his elder servant when he became an old man. He sent his servant to find a bride for his son Isaac, not from the local people but from his own land. So I'd tell them to be sure and seek God for your husband or wife. Don't do it yourself. Let Him appoint a person for you to marry and He will do it!"

"Here is the last question that I want to ask you: Has God stayed true to His Word for you?"

"Yes, of course He has! God is always true to His word. You know, we're the only ones that get sidetracked, but He's always true to His word, and what He promises He'll bring it to pass. But you know, sometimes, even though God stays true to His Word, sometimes we can miss it.

"Sometimes we can cause God's plans to be altered when we don't stay in line with the Word. We can cause it to be altered. You know, just like Sarah did when God promised Sarah and Abraham a son. Now see, God's plan wasn't for Hagar to have a child. That was to be between Sarah and her husband Abraham. But Sarah jumped in there and tried to give God a hand, as if He needed one.

"One of the reasons that it seems so long for Jesus to come back is because God's plans were altered so much during certain generations. They tried to help Him.

"In Hebrews, the tenth chapter and the thirty-fifth verse, it says, 'cast not away therefore your confidence,

The Bruce siblings on Easter Sunday, left to right:
Top row: Julianna, Isaac, Christine.
Bottom row: Rosalind, Demetrius, Joseph.

which has great recompense of reward.' In other words, let's wait on Him and be patient. Remember the Bible says we Christians walk by faith and not by sight.

"In Isaiah, I think its 55:11 where it says, 'So shall my word be that goeth forth out of my mouth: it shall not return unto me void, [but] it shall accomplish that which I please, and it shall prosper in the thing whereto I sent it' . . . you know, this is His word."

*Karetha Bruce outside
her Memphis home.*

CHAPTER SIX

Getting to Know You

"ISAAC, I THINK THIS MIGHT BE A GOOD PLACE FOR YOU TO ANSWER SOME OF YOUR FANS' QUESTIONS IF YOU DON'T MIND?"

"That's fine with me, but remember I might have to plead the Fifth on some of them," he says laughing.

"When you do get some time off, what kind of things do you like to do?"

Smiling, he says, "I'm a video game kinda guy. I mess around with them some. And John Madden! . . . You know that! I'm a big basketball fan, too. I like watching it; I like playing it. I think I'd probably watch a basketball game before I'd watch a football game."

"Do you get a chance to get out and see any NBA games?"

"Well, there's no NBA team in St. Louis, and I did go to school with Penny Hardaway at Memphis, and any time I can catch him, I do. We like to play video games and he's pretty good at them. I recently saw the Lakers and Minnesota play in Los Angeles. If I can get down to

Atlanta sometimes, I'll catch a Hawks game. I really liked watching the Chicago Bulls in their glory years when Michael [Jordan] was playing—I caught a couple of NBA finals games last year."

"Do you hang out with many of the Rams players these days?"

"The problem is a lot of my friends on the Rams have been released or signed with some other team, unfortunately. For a while, it was kind of hard to latch on to someone, and then they were gone. But that's the way with pro sports."

"Okay, I'll start off easy. How do you like St. Louis?"

"St. Louis is a great city. It's certainly a city that loves its sports, it loves its athletes, it's a great baseball town, great restaurants, and the schools are some of the best in the country."

"How about the new stadium, the Trans World Dome. Do you like it?"

"Its lovely! It's one of the better stadiums I've been in. I understand it was sort of modeled after the Georgia Dome in Atlanta and that's one of my favorite places. When I got a chance to compare ours, it ranked pretty high up there with me. It sure is a nice place to play."

"Is it a noisy place to play?"

"That's for sure. It was definitely loud."

"When you're spread out wide do you have a hard time hearing the snap count?"

"Most of the time I move on the ball. Sometimes I can anticipate the cadence and get a jump. I can pick up the cadence from Kurt. Once the play starts I don't hear a thing."

"Do you follow the baseball Cardinals?"

"Oh yeah, I'm always cheering for the Cardinals and I'm a big Mc fan. I read the sports page to see how they are doing and how many home runs he's hit."

"Have you had a chance to meet Mark McGwire yet?"

"Not yet but I hope to run across him someday soon."

"What is your favorite road stadium?"

"I think it would have to be the Georgia Dome. I've had a lot of success there. I also like playing in New Orleans, both places are real good."

"What is your least favorite stadium?"

"That has to be San Francisco by a mile with all that wind and fog. Their field is never the way it should be. Its soggy at one end, and the baseball field with all that dirt on the other end can get muddy. Sometimes the quarterbacks have a tough time throwing the ball when the wind catches it and that makes it hard for receivers. Running a route and catching a pass in San Francisco is a little bit like a batter trying to hit a knuckle ball pitch in baseball."

"What kind of relationship do you have with the media?"

"You know . . . I kinda let them do their job. I help them because I'm obligated to help them. I'm not mean or nasty. I know they've got a job to do just like I do, so I try not to be arrogant. I just go ahead and answer the questions that I'm asked and so be it. They're going to write what they want to write anyway."

"How do the Rams travel to away games?"

"We fly charter to all of our away games. Sometimes we might have a game where the wives or girlfriends can make the trip. With the Rams everything is always first class. That's what I like about playing with this organization."

"Tell me about the hotels you stay at when you're on the road. Are there always autograph seekers hanging around?"

"Again, we have great accommodations and yeah, its kinda the new thing . . . there are a lot more star players on the Rams now that the fans are looking to get their autographs, so that kind of evens things out for me."

"How did you feel the first time someone asked for your autograph?"

"I think that happened in college at Memphis, we had a promotion day, one of the media guys said that someone asked for my autograph, and that made me feel a little special. I could remember when I was a kid and got some of the Miami Dolphins' autographs, and I thought that was great. I didn't feel I was on the same level as those Dolphin players. Even today I don't feel that I'm on the exact same level as those guys I was asking for autographs from. You know its something special to me."

"If kids send you their Isaac Bruce football card to sign will you sign it and send it back?"

"Yes I do, and I get a bunch of those from all over the country. I really appreciate my fans."

"You were glad to be back in Los Angeles when the Rams drafted you but tell me how you felt when you learned the Rams were going to move to St. Louis?"

"I didn't know much about St. Louis. Like you said, I loved Los Angeles, I loved living out there, and I mean, the weather was just perfect. We did have a few true blue fans, but once the move was made it was out of my hands. So I just had to go with my job. Now that I've settled in here the team has had great success and I've had a good time being here and look forward to future blessings."

"Mike Martz is the new Rams head coach. How do you think he'll do?"

"He'll do fine. He was our offensive coordinator last season and if anyone can get us back to the Super Bowl it will be coach Martz. Remember he has great position coaches who put in long hard hours to bring the best out of us all."

"How often do you work out in the off season?"

"About four days out of the week. I do some running. But mostly I go to Dean Lotz's physical fitness center and work out. I don't spend a lot of time on pass catching in the off season . . . just enough to keep my timing sharp."

"Who do you work out with in the off season?"

"Dean Lotz was my college trainer at Memphis and now he's sort of my personal trainer. I've been with him ever since I've been in the league. He knows me real well. I work a lot on my quickness and I build up on that. I do endurance-type programs. I spend more time running the closer we get to opening training camp."

"Has this off season been any different with the Super Bowl win and all?"

"Somewhat. I've been asked to do more things this year. I have to pick and choose, and my agents at the Marketing Arm, Mark Clayton, Darin Perry, Jeff Chown, and several others do a good job in sorting things out for me. I've had to be a little more selective now, as I only have so much time to do things."

"Have you always worn number 80?"

"The Rams gave me that number when Henry Ellard left. In college at Memphis I was 83 but when I got to the Rams Flipper Anderson was 83 so I was 86 for a while."

"How do you feel the night before a game? Do you have any trouble sleeping?"

"Not at all, I sleep like a baby. I always have."

"What time do you wake up on game day?"

"I think I wake up pretty early. Sometimes we're required to check in to the stadium around 7:30 for a twelve o'clock game. I'm always up early. I shower and get dressed and lounge around the house then I head for the stadium.

"When do you go to the stadium?"

"I'm usually one of the first to arrive, around 7:30."

"When you come out of the locker room it has to be some kind of rush going out there in front of thousands of screaming fans. How do you keep calm with all the mayhem going on?"

"I know that's where the peace of God takes place in my life. He is Jehovah Shalom and I do ask for that peace and He is faithful to give us what we ask for. And that's the main part of having His peace."

"Are you starting to relax more as you get into the pre-game warm-up drills?"

"Yes. I've been that way for a long time. I would like to come out of the locker room and get it on because I'm nice and warm. Let's get it started!"

"Would you rather the Rams kick or receive to start the game?"

"I like to see us receive and get the ball. I'd like to get out early and put some points on the scoreboard."

"When do you feel you're into the game?"

"As soon as I run that first route and get some contact with the defenders, then I'm ready to get with it."

"What days do you have off and what do you like to do on your day off?'

"We have Mondays and Tuesdays off most of the time unless we're playing a game during the week. Now I'm a movie buff. Every Tuesday you can catch me at the theatre. Other than that I just relax and get my body ready to do it all over again."

"How does the snow and ice effect you in those cold November and December games played in outdoor stadiums?"

"It affects you a lot. I mean, it is definitely different for me, I was never used to playing in the cold. It does bother me. It's hard to get loose when it's freezing out there. It's really hard to open up and run but it's just something we have to go through."

"Do you watch much game film?

"Oh yeah! I watch film everyday up until game day. I try to figure my 'cans and cannots.' I want to know what are we going to be able to do against this team. Will it be more of a running game or more passing . . . that's what we want to get a handle on. From my perspective I want to get an idea who's going to be open and who are their best players on defense. That's basically what watching film is all about."

"When you're involved in a running play, like a flanker reverse, do you like carrying the ball?"

"Not really. Once in a while you break one for a large gain or a touchdown, and that's lovely, but many times the play doesn't go the way the receiver wants it to go. That linebacker that comes on a blitz and is sitting there waiting for you, he wants to get even with you for the times you burnt him."

"Do you read the sports page much?"

"Yeah, I do," laughing.

"What do you think about what is written about you?"

"I've sort of taken the attitude as far as the things I read about me, that I wished they knew me a little better. I believe it keeps me grounded no matter what anyone says about Isaac Bruce, good or bad, it won't change my way of thinking or swell my head up."

"Who is your favorite sports hero?"

"I like to see Barry Sanders who used to play with the Detroit Lions. I also like watching Jimmy Smith, from the Jacksonville Jaguars. Jimmy can run with the ball and he's an excellent receiver."

"I know many of the NFL and NBA players always seem to have a dress contest going on. What is your style of dress?"

"I wear a suit when it's required but at other times I'm just dressing casual, I like to be relaxed in what I wear so whatever is called for I can adapt."

"What kind of car do you drive?"

"I drive a Mercedes."

"Do you have a shoe contract?"

"Yes I have a contract with Nike."

"One thing I've noticed over the past few years is more and more players wearing gloves. I've even seen quarterbacks wear them sometimes. Can you catch as well with gloves or better with the bare hands?"

"I guess that depends on the individual. There are some guys who don't like wearing gloves, like Wayne Chrebet of the New York Jets. He doesn't wear them. I don't know, I used to be that way. I was to the point that I wanted to feel the ball, but then I started wearing the gloves and got them down to where I could feel the ball through the gloves. I just rough them up as best I can to be able to feel the football."

"What does Joseph think of his big brother? Are you his favorite player?"

Hesitating. "I honestly think I've made him proud of me. And he's made me proud of him, with the things he's done."

"What do you make of the gigantic salaries that professional athletes are receiving today? Do you think they are warranted?"

Again a bit hesitant. "I believe some of it is warranted. Then again we're playing a game that could be dangerous for the players. The life span of a professional ball player isn't too long. We're playing the sport that is entertaining and everyone loves. When we played in the big game, the Super Bowl, something like a billion people were watching it, which is amazing. I think the big salaries are right. We deserve to be paid for our part. You have a lot of owners making a bunch, but we never talk about their salaries. They do get to bring home a lot of money. And we only get a small portion of it. I think it's a blessing when you see what some of these guys get paid."

"How much did you sign for your first year?"

"I think it was a three-year contract for $1.5 million."

"I guess you are making a little more than that these days?"

Laughing, "Yeah, a little bit more."

"What's your favorite TV show?"

"I really like *Law and Order*, and I hate missing *Jeopardy* . . . it's sort of fun to match wits trying to answer the questions before the real contestants."

"What's your favorite movie?"

"I have two favorites, *What's Love Got to Do With It* about Tina Turner, and *A Few Good Men.* Those were two of my favorites."

"I like this one. What if the Isaac Bruce story were to be made into a movie, who do you see playing Isaac Bruce?"

"Wow, that's a tough one," he said chuckling. "Probably Omar Epps but I wouldn't rule out Denzel Washington."

"Are you hoping for a family in the future. How many kids would you like to have?"

"Oh yes! I'm looking forward to finding the wife the Lord brings to me and I hope to have one or maybe two kids."

"This is a tough question. How would you like to be remembered?"

Putting his hand to his chin he said, "I would like to be remembered as a man who helped people. To be remembered by the kids and those people that were around me, in the same city as me, I'll tell you this; I'm sure going to be remembered as a soldier of Jesus Christ! That's a given to me. Footballwise, I just want to be known as an intense receiver, because I don't think you find many of those. I want to be a guy that blocks and makes the plays."

"Isaac, I understand you have an excellent football camp during the summer. Where is that held?"

"It's held in Edwardsville, Illinois, at Southern Illinois University, and we have a bunch of NFL players on hand, and it's a very good learning experience for the kids. We have about five hundred kids in the camp and its one of my highlights of the off season."

"Thanks Isaac, and thank you fans for your questions. Well, Isaac, this has been fun for me. I hope it was the same for you?"

"Yes Jimmie, it was a lot of fun. I just hope my fans have a little better picture of me than they did before."

"I'm sure we can bet on that. I know its going to be hard to top the World Championship and catching the winning touchdown in the Super Bowl but I have a feeling if anyone can top it, it will be you!"

CHAPTER SEVEN

Waiting for the Draft

WHEN ISAAC'S COLLEGE DAYS WERE BEHIND HIM, IT BECAME TIME TO PLAY THE WAITING GAME LIKE THOUSANDS of other NFL hopefuls. He had put some good numbers up for the Tigers, 113 receptions for 1,586 yards and a big 15 touchdowns. But it's a long, impatient wait from December, when the college football season ends until April when the NFL holds its annual draft. This ritual has been going on ever sense the draft was instigated.

The rumor mill is always cranking at full speed during this time with stories of this player destined for New York, another to Green Bay, this guy's for sure being picked by Dallas, or the Jets are about ready to trade for the number one pick. Most of these stories are media inspired and not much more than the rumors they're said to be, but they can drive a prospective rookie up the walls. The only player who knows for sure where he'll be toiling come fall will be the "best college player available." He'll go to the worst team in the league as the NFL draft is set up with the team with the worst record picking first. Not your best destiny.

It was no different with Isaac Bruce. He thought for sure he would end up in either Pittsburgh or Seattle. Both had talked to him and assured him they were very interested in gaining his services. It didn't matter to him; he just wanted to play football somewhere.

He remembers a funny story about the time that a coach of the then Los Angeles Rams came to Memphis to look at game films of the Tigers. "The statement that got back to us was that they didn't like anybody on the team. Now here's the ironic part. When I was at Santa Monica JC, I went and saw the Rams practice scrimmage against the San Diego Chargers. That day I met John Becker, director of player personnel of the Rams. I guess I was about eighteen years old at the time and pretty impressed with all that was going on. He showed me a book that he was carrying around. He said this book listed all the college players that he was to look at that year for evaluating them. I remember telling myself right then and there, 'I've got to get into that book some kind of way!' And I guess I did and what was funny, it had to be three years later, after my two seasons at Memphis—John Becker was the same guy that drafted me."

Not only was Isaac in the Rams book, but he was also in a number of other teams' books. Several teams needing a player like himself had their eyes on this speedster from Florida by the way of California and Tennessee.

When he was drafted by the Rams in the second round he was happy to be going back to southern California where he had a good time at SMJC. It was almost full circle, at least for a while. The Rams were a team that hoped he could move in and give them good solid play at the wideout position, but not many people would have predicted the peaks that he has already reached in such a short period of time.

Reporting to the Rams training facility was an exciting experience for the young rookie. When asked if he could remember his first day at the Rams training camp he said, "Yeah. everything—everything I saw was just whizzing by so fast. I mean everything was just blurring my eyes. It took me about eight weeks to really know where I was. I didn't know how to make a team. I thought I made the team because I was a high second round draft pick. (Smiling) I really didn't have the mentality of an NFL wide receiver."

"Did the veterans give you rookies a hard time? Did you have to stand on the table and sing your school fight song?"

"Luckily, when I came out, Chuck Knox was the head coach, and he had issued a statement to the veterans to leave the rookies alone and that helped me a whole lot. I was still the guy who had to get the donuts in the morning, get the orange juice, carry the dummy pads in from practice. I was that guy. So I couldn't wait until my second year came around and someone else got the chores."

Was he nervous? Sure, who wouldn't be? Here you are a twenty-one-year-old about to embark on an adventure of a lifetime, one that few people ever have the opportunity to try. You feel like you are somewhere in between Indiana Jones and Hercules. You had to be physically tough and fast enough to outrun all those that were chasing you. Scared? Never! Isaac was sure that once the hitting started and he got the taste of what to expect at the NFL level, he'd be okay. It wasn't long before he was saying, "Okay, I'm ready to play, now give me the ball."

As usual Isaac didn't do anything humdrum—his first catch in the NFL was for a touchdown. Some way to start your career! "It was just a streak route. A nine route, just like in the Super Bowl. Chris Miller was the Rams quarterback at the time and he hit me deep in the end zone for a thirty-four-yard touchdown strike."

Most people remember his first year, 1994, as being his first all-pro season, but in reality in his first season he only caught twenty-one passes for 221 yards and three touchdowns. Not bad numbers for a rookie, but that was just the beginning.

The small crowds that came to see the lame duck Rams at Anaheim Stadium were something that didn't bother Isaac, because when he was in college Memphis didn't always fill up their stadium either. But he was glad to be back in Los Angeles even for a short time. The Rams would continue playing their home games that year in Anaheim.

He was also noticing that the step up from Division 1 football to the NFL was a much bigger jump than from junior college to the university level. He found at each level that the speed and size of the players seemed to increase at a tremendous rate. Linebackers that can run with wide receivers. Defensive linemen who can run down a running back. And defensive secondary players, both safeties and cornerbacks, are some of the fastest guys on the team. "Everybody's fast in the NFL—even a few quarterbacks!" he said smiling. "But one of the things that separated the good player from the great player was technique—just knowing how to use technique—being very conscious how you run routes, how you catch the ball, how you tuck it away, how you make one guy miss. . . . Technique, that is the separator."

Isaac had always been a good practice player to the point that he might have worked a little too hard, and too long. He practices as he plays, the only way he knows how—full out! "I think if I practice hard during the week, the games become easy for me."

By his second year, 1995, he was the Rams starting wideout. Enjoying his best season as a Ram, he caught 119 passes for 1,781 yards and 13 touchdowns. The accolades poured in, including being named to USA Today's All-Joe-team and the All-Madden team, honors that he's really proud of. He was given the Carroll Rosenbloom Memorial Award as the team's top rookie, the Daniel F. Reeves Memorial Award as the team's MVP, Fox's Terry Award for the best second-year pro, and he topped it all off with all-pro.

In just his third year, 1996, he had a breakout season, leading the Rams in receiving with 84 receptions and 1,338 yards, which was enough to also lead the league. He was the first Ram to do that since Henry Ellard did it in 1988. It was an exciting year, this second year in St. Louis. He was fast becoming the local fans' favorite and was fast becoming a national star. Again he was voted the team's MVP. This was only the second time that any Ram had won the award two years in a row. The others being DE Jack Youngblood and RB Eric Dickerson.

But the next season, 1997, brought the rough spots when nagging hamstring injuries curtailed his production to a low 56 receptions for 815 yards and five touchdowns. And he did that despite missing almost all of the first five games. For many NFL receivers this would be an outstanding year. Isaac also saw his streak of forty-three consecutive games with at least one reception snapped in Denver after leaving the game in the first quarter with a pulled hamstring.

The numbers he put up were even more astonishing when you consider missing all those games. By most standards what he did would make most receivers very happy. He ranked third in team scoring, recorded two 100-yard games, and, in Atlanta, he recorded another Rams record-catching 10 passes for 233 yards and 2 touchdowns. This was enough to lead the NFL, and was the fourth highest receiving production for any Ram. He was the only player in the team's long and colorful history to have three games with at least two hundred yards, and only the seventh in NFL history to do so. He is the only Ram to record three games with two hundred yards. He ended the troubled year in New Orleans in typical Isaac Bruce style, catching a five-yard, game-winning touchdown pass from Tony Banks, who was the Rams quarterback.

Hoping that 1998 would see the injuries behind him, he soon found it wasn't to be. The old nemesis, injured hamstrings, would continue to haunt him.

The season started off with great expectations as he opened it where he had left off in New Orleans, catching 10 passes for 131 yards. He bettered that the next week with 11 receptions for 192 yards and one touchdown, and that was against the defending NFC (National Football Conference) champs, the Minnesota Vikings. The fans had created a rivalry between the Vikings rookie wide receiver Randy Moss, who would go on and garner rookie of the year honors, and Isaac. The year saw him make a catch for eighty yards and a TD. Despite missing eight games he still accounted for 32 receptions for 457 yards. He was placed on the injured reserve list again on December 7.

Those around the country who only a short time back were calling him the heir apparent to the great Jerry Rice of the San Francisco 49ers were now about to write him off as a flash in the pan. He would notice this most when he would enter or leave the field to head up the gangway to the locker room where fans just a few games back were all yelling, "Isaac, Isaac" . . . now those same people were yelling, "you're too soft Bruce," "toughen up," and some other things best left unsaid.

When asked about being compared to Rice he responded, "Well, you know I have great respect for Jerry Rice—not only his game, which is in a league by itself, but as a person who has always conducted himself as a gentleman. There are lots of guys out there like Michael Irvin, Andre Risen, Henry Ellard, and more. There were guys I watched growing up like Nate Moore, Mark Clayton, Duper, Lynn Swann—but I didn't want to come into the NFL with a label on me. I think one of the main reasons they put that label on me was that we both wear number 80. I don't want a label; I just want to be the first Isaac Bruce. And I hope that doesn't sound arrogant because it is not meant that way."

One of the things all young professionals go through when they break into professional sports is a kind of awe when for the first time they are on the same playing field with the heroes that they've grown up watching—and not knowing how to act. They've seen them play on television, collected their trading cards, and sought their autographs—but now here they are playing with them or against them!

"You know, when you walk out onto that field for the first time and there they are—in real life—your heroes, it makes you a young fan again. I remember the first time it happened to me . . . we were playing San Francisco and Joe Montana was their quarterback. There I was, standing next to our head coach, watching the game as a fan, and not really playing in it. I remember watching Montana and Jerry Rice perform and do their jobs that they've been so great at all these years. This one time Montana was knocked out of bounds. He was kind of right there at my feet, and I reached out and touched him, because I wanted to touch a legend."

Isaac always tries to learn from all the great receivers in the NFL. He always looks for that something, that little edge that will make him the best. He is even taking pride in his blocking these days.

He was already looking forward to the 1999 season before it started.

CHAPTER EIGHT

Getting Ready for 1999

THE 1999 NFL FOOTBALL SEASON WAS JUST A FEW SHORT WEEKS AHEAD WHEN ISAAC REPORTED TO THE RAMS SUMMER CAMP facility at Southern Illinois University in Edwardsville. Arriving with the other veterans in the hot, muggy days of early July in the Midwest, he was ready to put the fable that the career of Isaac Bruce was finished behind him. He had heard the crowds for the last two seasons call him a slacker, that he had become soft. But he was healed and he planned to stay healed! He was taking no chances with his valuable legs. But he was ready to have fun again after a couple of seasons that were far from fun! His faith was stronger than ever, and he could hardly wait to get started.

He had the attitude that this was going to be a "big-time season." His motto, "If I'm well, I'm hell" became "If I'm well, I'm hell—and, I'm well."

Isaac was also excited about being reunited with his old receivers coach Mike Martz from the Washington

Redskins where he had served as Norv Turner's quarter-back coach. He had been the Rams receivers' coach for two years under head coach Rich Brooks. Isaac had his best years under Martz's tutelage.

Martz would be taking over the job as offensive coordinator replacing Jerry Rhome. In Washington, Martz never had the quality players that he would have to work with in St. Louis, and he was excited about the upcoming season. "This is the most fun that I've had in my coaching career. It's really exciting, with the type of people that we have on the staff, the players we have, the quality of athletes that we have. It's an exciting time for me and I can't wait to get this thing cranked up!"

He had nothing but praise for his former pupil. "Well, he's done it all. He's been the best, and he's lined up against the very best in this league and worn them out, and there's just no substitute for that."

Isaac was one too that handed out some accolades when quoted in Bernie Miklasz's column in the *St. Louis Post Dispatch* in July of '99. He said, "Coach Saunders, the Rams receivers coach, and Coach Martz, they really stress quality. Quality is important to me. I didn't know how important it was until those types of guys weren't here. Quality isn't going out there to just run around all day. I've learned the true meaning of quality. Quality is what matters in this game."

"Coach Martz knows his stuff. I had it going when he was my receiver's coach. He had the true idea of how to get someone open . . . And good coaching is, when you critique, please, give me another way out. Don't just tell me not to do something a certain way, or that I'm doing something wrong and then leave me in limbo to figure things out. Tell me how to do it better. Help me attack the problem and find a solution. Coach Saunders and Coach Martz, that's what they do."

When asked about Isaac's past two injury-riddled seasons and what he thought the chances that his star would be back in good health, Martz said, "Speaking about the past two years with all the injuries, I hope that's all behind him. We had a little bit of a scare during mini-camp, where he tore or stretched some scar tissue, but since then he's been fine."

Again Miklasz said, "The movement to save Bruce's legs is underway. The coaches monitor him carefully, and put up the stop sign when he reaches an assigned number of pass routes each day.

"Bruce knows this medicine is good for him, even if he doesn't like the taste. He says he doesn't want his teammates to think that he isn't willing to work as hard as they are. But he's adjusted."

It was a good day for the Rams when they picked Torry Holt out of North Carolina State as the sixth player taken in the '99 draft. Not only was Holt the kind of young man that Isaac could take to, he was also the kind of player that could take some of the heat off him. Along with Az-zahir Hakim, Ricky Proehl, and Marshall Faulk coming out of the backfield as a great receiver, it could mean some long days ahead for the opponent's secondary.

The preseason camp went well for Isaac with very little problem with his hamstring. The Rams had a so-so preseason with a 2–2 record, but Isaac turned in a very respectable 147 yards on 7 catches, giving him a 21.0 average per reception. His longest was 52 yards and a touchdown. He also registered a solo tackle!

Trent Green, who came over from the Washington Redskins, would be at quarterback and he was one who

Isaac respected a great deal. Green had come to the Rams as a free agent from the Redskins. He went down with a knee injury during the second preseason game. This injury would put him out of action for the rest of the season. It would have been easy for the Rams to take the attitude of "there goes the season" when their leader went down. When asked if that was the attitude that he felt, Isaac said, "Not really, I didn't. I still believed we would have a good season, something special. I never lost faith. But when I saw Trent go down, I think I was more, you know, 'wow, this is my friend right here, who's been preparing so hard for this position as our quarterback and leader for this time in his life, right here. And now here he is lying down with his knee all busted up.' I felt more like I lost a friend on the field, rather than just a teammate."

Many times when a player is hurt it opens the door for someone to come in and try to fill that spot. No player likes to earn his job by someone else's misfortune but that's the way things are in professional sports.

A young rookie named Kurt Warner from Northern Iowa University was given the task of leading the Rams and, with his faith in God and his teammates, what a dream season he had! When Isaac was asked what he thought was a big part in Warner's success, Isaac said, "I think his belief in God was the biggest part of his success. Without a doubt! And I'm sure he'd tell you the same thing. Plus, he believes in himself. He knows he can get the job done and he does! He's so calm out there. I think the reason for that is he really doesn't need to be antsy about anything. When you look in the huddle, and you see all the guys who can make big plays and who can block for you, there's really no need to be antsy about anything."

With the preseason over the team was getting ready for the opening-day game of the regular 1999 season in St. Louis on September 12 at the Trans World Dome against the Baltimore Ravens. It was a balmy day outside but inside temperature was a warm 72 degrees, and a paid attendance of 62,100 screaming fans filled the stadium, all with high hopes, as all fans do throughout the league on opening day.

With a rookie quarterback, one rookie wide receiver, a new running back, and hopefully a healthy Isaac Bruce the team was anxious to get the 1999 season underway and see just how good they could be!

The team broke camp at the beginning of August and Isaac moved into his condo in Creve Coure to wait for a season of what he had always dreamed of. Was it to be? He spent the week running errands, getting ticket requests filled, and just trying to relax. "I never have much trouble relaxing," he said. "I just try to have God's peace."

After a great night's sleep the night before the first game, Isaac was anxious to get to the stadium and get dressed. He drove his Mercedes the short ten minute drive from his condo to the Trans World Dome, checking in about 7:30. He would get taped and have any injuries treated, bandaged, and everything else NFL trainers do to put a healthy football player on the field. It was no easy task for head trainer Jim Anderson and his assistants Ron Dubuque and Dake Walden. With forty-five well-tuned, very talented, and very valuable properties to take care of, it couldn't be an easy task, but they always manage the impossible.

The short drive seemed longer than it should have, but that was just the adrenaline starting to flow. The brain was on total recall, sorting through the past weeks' practices and the game plan for the Ravens. He was wondering who he would be going up against, in case they tried to surprise the Rams healthy speedster. Finally the trip was over and it was time to take care of the business at hand.

Asked if he had any routine that he went through on game day Isaac answered, "No, not really, I don't do the same things, I switch off to various things but I just never got into the routine thing. That's just the way I am."

Finally the moment he had been waiting for. Would the hamstrings hold up? Was this going to be a season like the past two? Would he be his old self? Was the special treatment he had given his legs worthwhile? Or would he have another year of trials? He knew what he could do as a player! He knew down deep inside what he could do. He makes things happen when he's on the field, he always makes something happen. He was ready to play sixteen games this season. His faith was greater than ever.

The first game is always something special to the coaches and players. All teams start the season with a clean slate, no wins and no losses. It gives you a chance to match up against other NFL players and put all that hard work from the hot summer camp into an all out effort. The excitement builds until the first kick off and that first series of downs is underway.

Game One

The Ravens would be no match for the multi-talented St. Louis team. The Rams wasted no time in getting on the scoreboard early in the first quarter when placekicker Jeff Wilkins, the veteran in his fifth year out of Youngstown State, kicked a thirty-six-yard field goal.

Rams 3, Ravens 0

The field goal was followed quickly by Kurt Warner's first touchdown pass of the afternoon to Roland Williams, the big 6'5" 270-pound tight end out of Syracuse. The pass only covered six yards but this was one small step to what would end up being a record setting year. Warner had a big day completing 28 of 44 passes for 308 yards.

Rams 14, Ravens 0

The Ravens came back to get three points on Matt Stover's 25-yard field goal to tie the score.

Rams 14, Ravens 3

But now it was Isaac's turn to get into the end zone with a two-yard scoring pass from Warner with 33 seconds left in the half. His eight receptions and 92 yards were team highs. He was tied for fifth in the NFC with the eight catches at the end of the first game.

Rams 17, Ravens 3

Baltimore cut the lead to 17–10 with fifteen seconds to go in the third quarter when QB Scott Mitchell hit WR Brandon Stokley for a twenty-eight-yard touchdown. They weren't going to give up without a fight.

Rams 17, Ravens 10

Wilkins hit on his second field goal; a booming fifty-one yarder gave the Rams a 20–10 lead with 8:56 to go in the contest.

Rams 20, Ravens 10

Warner threw his third touchdown pass of the day to rookie wide receiver Torry Holt who scored his first NFL touchdown on the twenty-yard aerial. He would record three receptions for thirty-six yards and an average of twelve yards per carry. All aspects of the Rams game were running well. The offense, the defense, and the special teams all contributed. The final score was Rams 27–Ravens 10. It certainly pleased head coach Dick Vermeil to see his charges get off to a flying start.

Final Score: Rams 27, Ravens 10

Isaac ended up as the leading receiver in the game with eight catches for ninety-two yards and one touchdown. The best part, his hamstrings held up!

Isaac's Comments

When asked how he would rate the Ravens defense he answered, "I think they had the best defensive player in the league in Ray Lewis. He was everywhere! He made a lot of big plays, and they played together. They did have a good, strong defense.

"I felt the Baltimore game was a good start for me considering I had missed eleven games the previous season. So, I was happy to get back out there and get back in the groove of things. I felt great!"

"Did Kurt Warner's fast start, throwing three touchdown passes in his first NFL regular season game, come as a surprise to you?"

"No, it didn't surprise me . . . like I said earlier, we had a lot of talent on the team, a lot of talent on offense to help him. We were there to support him, and he did his job like we all felt he would. He showed up!"

Isaac did well averaging eight yards per catch . . . that tied him for fifth in the NFC. His eight receptions and ninety-two yards were both team highs.

THE START OF SOMETHING BIG

Team	Receptions	Yards	Touchdowns
Baltimore	8	92	1
Season Total	8	92	1

Won 1   Lost 0

CHAPTER NINE

A One-Game Winning Streak

THE RAMS HAD MONDAY AND TUESDAY OFF, AS WAS THE NORMAL SCHEDULE AFTER A WINNING EFFORT. EVEN SO THERE WAS AN electrically charged atmosphere at the Rams training facility in St. Louis. When the players came in early Wednesday morning, each one of them was happily basking in the total team victory over the Baltimore Ravens.

However, they all knew that not much time would be allotted for celebration, because they had to prepare for the game against the defending National Football League Champions, the Atlanta Falcons, on Sunday in St. Louis. After all, there would be 63,253 devoted Rams fans on hand, and these players never wanted to let their fans down.

This wasn't the same Falcon team that represented the NFC in Super Bowl XXXIII. Chris Chandler, the Falcon's quarterback, was having hamstring problems and couldn't maneuver enough to get away from the fired-up Rams defense.

Game Two

The Rams started the game off with a seventeen-play, eighty yard, ten minute and thirteen second drive that culminated with running back Robert Holcombe going over from the one-yard line for the first score of the day. Holcombe out of Illinois had lots of friends on hand to see this third-year man run and catch the ball.

Rams 7, Falcons 0

After forcing Atlanta to punt, Warner connected with wide receiver Torry Holt for a thirty-eight-yard touchdown on St. Louis's first play of the second quarter. Holt had now caught touchdown passes in his first two NFL games.

Rams 14, Falcons 0

Then on the first play of Atlanta's next possession, corner back Todd Lyght intercepted a Chandler pass and returned it eighteen yards. On the ensuing play, Kurt Warner hit Isaac with a forty-six-yard touchdown strike. At this point Isaac Bruce was the Rams receiving leader with 160 yards.

Rams 21, Falcons 0

As always, it continued to be a team effort. Marshall Faulk had rushed for 105 yards on seventeen carries and he had caught five passes for sixty-seven yards. This was his first one hundred-yard game of the season, and his fifteenth career one hundred-yard rushing game. So Faulk next came back with a reception from Warner that he took into the end zone from seventeen yards out for the touchdown. That play ranked Marshall Faulk fifth in the NFC with 298 total yards from scrimmage.

Rams 28, Falcons 0

Just before the half, Tony Graziani replaced Chris Chandler at quarterback after Chandler injured his hamstring a second time. Graziani then moved the Falcons down the field for their only scoring drive, hitting tight end Brian Kozlowski with a one-yard toss for the touchdown. The Falcons then successfully put up the extra point.

Rams 28, Falcons 7

Isaac caught only three passes on the day, but one of them was for forty-six-yards and a touchdown. To close out the game, the rookie quarterback Warner ran it in from the five-yard line for his first rushing NFL touchdown. It was the second straight game in which Warner had thrown three touchdown passes. He became the second quarterback in fifty years to throw three touchdowns in his first two NFL games. Only the great Dan Marino of the Miami Dolphins had accomplished such a feat before. Now Kurt Warner was ranked second among all NFL quarterbacks for the season. Only Brad Johnson of the Washington Redskins with a 65.2 completion percentage and a 108.6 quarterback rating was ahead of him.

Final Score: Rams 35, Falcons 7

ISAAC'S RECORD AT THIS POINT IN THE SEASON

Team	Receptions	Yards	Touchdowns
Baltimore	8	92	1
Atlanta	3	68	1
Season Total	11	160	2

Won 2   Lost 0

When asked, what in the world could bring down a team from the top of the division where the Falcons had been to a team that was floundering? Isaac's response was, "I think that when the Falcons traded . . . I mean they released Tony Martin that was a big, big mistake. He was their number one downfield threat and another factor was Jamal Anderson going down with a knee injury."

The Rams were looking to go up 3–0 when they went into Cinergy Field on October 3 to play the Cincinnati Bengals. A paid attendance of 45,481 was mostly Cincinnati fans, but a large group from St. Louis had made the trip to see their heroes who had shown such promise in the early going. National television exposure had the country wondering if they were for real.

The sky was sunny and the temperature was a football-perfect 65 degrees. It was a big day again for the offense. WR Az-zahir Hakim tied a Rams scoring record by pulling down four touchdowns in one game. (Three on passes and one on an eighty-four-yard punt return. On the punt, he actually dropped the ball and picked it up and went the distance.) WR Harold Jackson was the last Ram to accomplish this feat in 1973 against the Dallas Cowboys.

Isaac had his best day of the young season, catching six passes for 152 yards. Even though he didn't get into the end zone he drew such coverage all day that the other receivers were able to get free. He recorded his nineteenth one hundred-yard receiving game. His 152 yards was the second highest total for the season.

In this game Warner became the first quarterback to throw three touchdown passes in his first three starts in the NFL. Completing 17 of 21 passes for 310 yards gave him a quarterback rating of 158.3, the highest possible rating for a quarterback with at least twenty attempts.

Game Three

Cincinnati scored on it's opening drive of the game on a thirty-six-yard field goal by Doug Pelfrey. This would be the only time they would hold the lead in the game.

Rams 0, Bengals 3

But the Rams didn't like being behind and only took three minutes to go ahead as Warner hit Az-zahir Hakim, the second-year wide receiver out of San Diego State, on a nine-yard play. Hakim is also one of the premier punt returners in the NFL.

Rams 7, Bengals 3

Then FB Robert Holcombe bulled over from the one-yard line to extend the Rams' lead.

Rams 14, Bengals 3

After the Bengals failed to get anything going they were forced to punt to the Rams. Then it was time again for Hakim to go deep as Warner connected on a fifty-one-yard pass that the fleet Hakim took in and just blew by the defenders for the score.

Rams 21, Bengals 3

Cincinnati was just no match for the powerful Rams who were excelling in every area.

The Hakim show continued when Cincinnati was forced to punt on fourth down. Hakim had trouble fielding the ball, but when he picked it up he scampered eighty-four yards for the touchdown. The eighty-four-yard return was fifth best in the Rams' history.

Rams 28, Bengals 3

Hakim scored his fourth and final touchdown, an eighteen-yard pass from Warner. All three of his receptions went for touchdowns.

Rams 35, Bengals 3

Akili Smith, the rookie quarterback from the University of Oregon, scored the only Cincinnati touchdown on a one-yard run with 2:26 left in the game.

Rams 35, Bengals 10

Jeff Wilkins hit a nineteen-yard field goal to finish the scoring.

Final Score: Rams 38, Bengals 10

Isaac's Comments

"Oh, I felt great about it . . . we were playing Cincinnati and some of the so-called sportswriters had predicted we would lose the game. Because they didn't think we were ready to play or that the Bengals could sneak up on us but it just didn't happen. When the sportswriters, especially your hometown writers say something negative you just want to go out there and make them eat their words. We played well as a complete unit together. Along with Az-zahir Hakim having a great day."

Isaac led all receivers with six receptions for 152 yards averaging a heavy 25.3 yards per catch. Against the Bengals he recorded his nineteenth one hundred-yard game. He was tied for sixth in the NFC.

NOW ISAAC'S RECORD WAS

Team	Receptions	Yards	Touchdowns
Baltimore	8	92	1
Atlanta	3	68	1
Cincinnati	6	152	0
Season Total	17	312	2

Won 3   Lost 0

The Rams took their record to 4–0 for the first time since 1995 and equaled their win total for all of 1998 by downing the once powerful San Francisco 49ers at the Trans World Dome before a paid crowd of 65,872 jubilant fans.

Kurt Warner tied another Rams record by throwing five touchdowns in one game. (He also had four other games with at least three touchdown passes.)

The game with the 49ers was also a record setting day for Isaac as he had another big day with five receptions for 134 yards and four touchdowns. Not bad for only five receptions! Those four TD's tied a Rams team record.

Game Four

The Rams got onto the scoreboard first when Warner hit Isaac with a thirteen-yard strike and his first touchdown of the game.

Rams 7, 49ers 0

The 49ers were without their all-pro quarterback, Steve Young who had taken a few shots to the head and was being sidelined for medical evaluation. Jeff Garcia, a rookie even though he had played six years in the Canadian Football League, was given the starting job off of what had been a pretty good preseason.

After the Rams got the ball back the next drive was not much different than the first with Kurt Warner hitting Isaac with a five-yard scoring toss with 4:26 still left in the first quarter. Isaac's catch was just part of a very big day by the speed burner from the University of Memphis.

Rams 14, 49ers 0

With one of the few drives that San Francisco could put together, the 49ers finally got on the scoreboard when Wade Richey booted a forty-two-yard field goal.

Rams 14, 49ers 3

Getting great field position after a fifty-four-yard kickoff return by Torry Holt, St. Louis again went to the air with Warner hitting Isaac again on a forty-five-yard streak pattern for the touchdown with one minute and twelve seconds left in the first quarter. The Bruce-Warner combo made it look easy.

Rams 21, 49ers 3

San Francisco scored on their first drive of the second quarter when Lawrence Phillips out of the University of Nebraska, the much talked about running back and former Ram, ran in the ball from the two-yard line for the touchdown.

Rams 21, 49ers 10

St. Louis went up 28–10 when Warner hit TE Jeff Robinson from the University of Idaho, for twenty-two-yards and the touchdown. It was his first scoring reception of the season and his second career touchdown.

Rams 28, 49ers 10

On one of the few occasions when the big offensive line let someone get to their young quarterback, blitzing safety Tim McDonald hit Warner who fumbled the ball into the end zone. Junior Bryant, the 49er all-pro defensive tackle, made the recovery for the TD.

Rams 28, 49ers 17

Richey hit on his second field goal of the day, a forty-three yarder to cut the Rams' lead to just eight points, but the Rams, with their exciting speedsters, were far from through. Torry Holt continued to have his afterburners fired up as he returned the kickoff for ninety-seven yards and the score. Holt also caught three passes for sixty-seven yards. This was the kind of play that demoralizes a team that was fighting back and then, boom, the roof falls in!

Rams 35, 49ers 20

Then Isaac made his record tying catch, reeling in a forty-two-yard pass from Warner with 11:10 still remaining in the final quarter. Another one hundred-plus yard day, and the wheels were staying on. He was feeling good about everything.

Final Score: Rams 42, 49ers 20

Isaac's Comments

"I think one thing that helped was I didn't complain about not catching any touchdown passes in the previous game against Cincinnati. I thanked God for what he had allowed me to accomplish against the Bengals and He came right back and proved Himself again. It was a big game, and all of us—and I mean all of us—were ready to play that game.

"One thing most people don't realize is even though the Rams have moved to St. Louis, and there's no longer a southern California vs. northern California rivalry. . . .

It's still the Rams vs. the 49ers. You can't imagine how big that game is! It's a war!"

ISAAC'S CONTINUING RECORD

Team	Receptions	Yards	Touchdowns
Baltimore	8	92	1
Atlanta	3	68	1
Cincinnati	6	152	0
San Francisco	5	134	4
Season Total	22	446	6

Won 4   Lost 0

Isaac had a career high four touchdown receptions and put his twentieth one hundred-yard game in the books. He moved into the number one spot for receivers in the NFC and second behind Glenn from New England in the NFL with six touchdown receptions.

CHAPTER TEN

Winning Ways Continue

THE RAMS CONTINUED THEIR WINNING WAYS AS THEY RACKED UP THEIR FIFTH STRAIGHT VICTORY, BEATING THE ATLANTA Falcons and making this the first 5–0 season since 1989. The entire team was fired up because this was the second meeting of the season between the Rams and the Falcons, but this time it would be played in the Georgia Dome before 51,973 fans who wanted their Falcons to turn things around and get back on the winning track of the previous championship year.

But the game showed the Rams improving in almost every aspect of the game. The score of 41–13 marked the second consecutive game that the Rams had scored more than 40 points.

Marshall Faulk had a great day running the ball for 181 yards on eighteen carries and catching three passes for thirty-one yards giving him 212 all-purpose yards for the day. After coming off a six-yard game on seven carries the week before, he was elated to be back running like he knew he could.

 # Game Five

The combination of Warner to Bruce was fast becoming the Tinkers to Evers to Chance of the NFL, as the quarterback hit his famed wide receiver for a four-yard touchdown with just a little over five minutes gone in the game. Isaac was fourth in the league in receptions with twenty-eight.

Rams 7, Falcons 0

Then Marshall Faulk ran in from six yards for another score. This big day would move him into the sixth spot in the NFL in rushing with 502 yards.

Rams 14, Falcons 0

Atlanta got on the board with 11:19 left in the first half when QB Chris Chandler hit FB Bob Christian for a thirteen-yard touchdown.

Rams 14, Falcons 7

On the ensuing kickoff Tony Horne, the rookie from Clemson, quickly showed the NFL that he was no fluke as he returned the kick 101 yards for a touchdown. With this scoring run it made it two weeks in a row that he had returned a kickoff for a touchdown. His longest scoring return was in 1998, his rookie season when he went 102 yards against the same Atlanta Falcons.

Rams 21, Falcons 7

It was time for the Rams' defense to get in on the scoring with 1:42 left in the half when LB Mike Jones tipped Chandler's pass that found its way into the open hands of DE Grant Wistrom. The 6'4" 270-pounder outran every one, going ninety-one yards and getting the touchdown. It was the longest interception return by a defensive lineman in team history.

Rams 28, Falcons 7

With thirty-two seconds left in the first half, Morten Andersen kicked a nineteen-yard field goal to give the Falcons three points.

Rams 28, Falcons 10

When the second half got under way it was time for St. Louis kicker Jeff Wilkins to put a twenty-two-yard field goal through the uprights. His attempt was successful.

Rams 31, Falcons 10

Then Wilkins kicked another three pointer this time from forty-nine yards out to increase the Rams' lead.

Rams 34, Falcons 10

St. Louis completed a successful drive by adding one more touchdown. FB Robert Holcombe ran in the ball from the one yard line.

Rams 41, Falcons 10

Morten Andersen hit on a twenty-five-yard field goal to end the scoring for the day.

Final Score: Rams 41, Falcons 13

Again Isaac was the leading receiver with forty-eight yards on six receptions and one TD.

Isaac's Comments

"I don't know what their problem is. I know they've had a lot of key people hurt and that always creates a problem for a team. We were able to take advantage of their injuries. We had a great day running the ball. Marshall put up a lot of big numbers on the ground [181 yards]."

HIS RECORD THEN LOOKED LIKE THIS

Team	Receptions	Yards	Touchdowns
Baltimore	8	92	1
Atlanta	3	68	1
Cincinnati	6	152	0
San Francisco	5	134	4
Atlanta	6	48	1
Season Total	28	494	7

Won 5   Lost 0

Another St. Louis Rams milestone came on October 24 of that year when the Cleveland Browns came to the Trans World Dome to meet the charging Rams. But after all, it was just another good day for St. Louis as the Rams scored over thirty points for the fourth time in the year. No Rams team since 1989 had gone 6–0.

110

Game Six

TE Roland Williams opened the scoring for St. Louis when he caught a one-yard toss from Kurt Warner. This would keep alive Warner's string of at least one touchdown pass in each game.

Rams 7, Browns 0

Marshall Faulk had another big game, rushing for 133 yards on sixteen tries. One of those being a dazzling thirty-three-yard run. He also caught nine passes for sixty-seven yards.

Rams safety Devin Bush lowered the boom on Cleveland WR Ronnie Powell, forcing him to fumble the ball, and LB Charlie Clemons recovered on the St. Louis twenty-eight-yard line.

It was a relatively slow day for Isaac as he caught four passes for forty-four yards. But he continued to connect with Warner and got the second score of the day on a four-yard pass. The reception made it eight touchdown catches for the season, placing him second in the NFC in receiving yards.

Rams 14, Browns 0

The Browns kicker made a forty-seven-yard field goal to put the Cleveland team on the scoreboard.

Rams 14, Browns 3

Throwing again for his third touchdown in the game, Warner found TE Roland Williams open for a one yard TD. The Rams QB had thrown three or more touchdowns in five out of six games. He led the NFL with eighteen touchdown passes and a quarterback rating of 131.6. He also led the NFL with an average of 9.45 yards gained per pass.

Rams 21, Browns 3

Jeff Wilkins came back with his first field goal of the day to add to the Rams' lead.

Rams 24, Browns 3

Then another Faulk run of thirty-three yards put the Rams way out in front. He finished the day with the second consecutive game with two hundred total yards from the line of scrimmage.

Rams 31, Browns 3

Wilkins finished up the scoring by hitting his second field goal of the day.

Final Score: Rams 34, Browns 3

Isaac's Comments

"Roland Williams caught another touchdown pass. He's starting to get a few and he's not about to let you forget it. I'll tell you this; he's one outstanding blocker. He prides himself with his blocking."

After making two catches for touchdowns Isaac was asked if trying to get free from the five-yard line is more difficult than say from the forty-yard line he said, "It is harder. First of all you can't run any deep patterns because you just don't have the field. Also the defense tightens up when we get down there."

"Is the hitting any harder down close?"

Smiling, he answered, "The hitting is always pretty good, especially if they catch you with one."

ISAAC'S CONTINUED RECORD

Team	Receptions	Yards	Touchdowns
Baltimore	8	92	1
Atlanta	3	68	1
Cincinnati	6	152	0
San Francisco	5	134	4
Atlanta	6	48	1
Cleveland	4	44	1
SEASON TOTAL	32	538	8

Won 6   Lost 0

113

CHAPTER ELEVEN

America's Team?

THE RAMS WERE FEELING PRETTY GOOD ABOUT THEMSELVES, AND THE REST OF THE COUNTRY WAS FEELING PRETTY GOOD ABOUT them too. Several weeks of running up high scores with big exciting plays on national television was fast creating a new "America's Team" with athletes that could do so many things well. The young quarterback, Kurt Warner, was tying or setting records with each new game. How long could this run last? That was the question.

And Isaac too was off to a sensational season and also on a league-leading pace. Torry Holt, Marshall Faulk, and Az-zahir Hakim and the big offensive line were looking like giant killers.

But win number seven would have to wait a while. The Rams ventured into the new Adelphia Coliseum on October 31 to meet the Tennessee Titans. It was a balmy, sunny day with the temperature hovering around 76 degrees when the fired up Titans handed them their first defeat of the season in a close game 24–21. Though it was Halloween, this was no trick or treat.

Kurt Warner had another three-touchdown-pass game but Titan quarterback Steve McNair was up to the task also. Passing for two touchdowns and running for one, he kept his team in the game until they could hit on an Al Del Greco field goal to put them on top to stay.

Isaac again added to his touchdown total pulling in a three-yard toss from Warner.

Tennessee had a big first quarter scoring twenty-one points before the Rams could do much of anything.

 # Game Seven

The Titans scored on the first drive of the game and this would set the tempo for most of the first three quarters. McNair finished an eighty-yard, eleven-play drive with a one-yard pass to FB Lorenzo Neal for the touchdown.

Rams 0, Titans 7

Still in the first quarter, Tennessee linebacker Joe Bowden sacked the St. Louis quarterback who fumbled the ball. Titan linebacker Barron Wortham fell on it. On the very next play from scrimmage, McNair hit Eddie George, with a seventeen-yard completion for the touchdown.

Rams 0, Titans 14

Things did not get better for the Rams as on the next possession Warner fumbled and LB Wortham recovered the ball on the St. Louis twenty-six-yard line. Two plays later McNair scored on a ten-yard run with 1:24 left in the first quarter.

Rams 0, Titans 21

With their backs against the wall it didn't take the Rams long to get back in gear. On the second play of the third quarter Warner completed a short pass to Marshall Faulk who turned that short pass into a dazzling fifty-seven-yard touchdown run, going around and over tacklers.

Rams 7, Titans 21

Still in the third quarter the Rams were able to score when Warner hit Isaac on a three-yard pass. This culminated a six-play, fifty-nine-yard scoring drive. Isaac made his ninth touchdown catch, the thirty-eighth of his short career. The nine receptions to this point gave him the NFC lead, and he was tied with Marvin Harrison of the Colts for the top spot in the NFL.

Rams 14, Titans 21

With the Rams coming back strong the Titans were not done yet as Al Del Greco came in and booted a twenty-seven-yard field goal to extend the lead.

Rams 14, Titans 24

It was late in the fourth quarter when St. Louis put together an eleven-play, eighty-yard drive that ended when Warner found RB Amp Lee, the much traveled veteran from Florida State, for a fifteen-yard score. This was his first score of the year.

Final Score: Rams 21, Titans 24

St. Louis then tried an onside kickoff and it was recovered by Rams' linebacker Lorenzo Styles on the St. Louis forty-two-yard line. The Rams were not about to give up as Warner drove the Rams to the Tennessee twenty-yard line with seven seconds left in the game. This set up a thirty-eight-yard field goal attempt by Jeff Wilkins hoping to tie the game and send it into overtime, but the kick sailed wide right and closed the door on win number seven.

Warner, despite the fumble and the loss of the ball on a sack, still managed a game that most quarterbacks can only dream of. He completed twenty-nine of forty-six passes for a career high of 328 yards and three touchdowns.

Warner led the NFL in touchdown passes (twenty-one) and completion percentage (70.7). He had not thrown an interception in 107 passes. Warner also tied a modern-day record with Bret Favre of the Green Bay Packers for the most touchdown passes thrown in the first seven games of the season with twenty-one.

Isaac's Comments

"I think that was the first time that Kurt showed that it was his first year starting at quarterback. They were hitting him pretty good, you know. When you're getting hit, it's hard to play your type of game, when you're getting tagged on every single play.

"I think the Titans had a great scheme for us and it worked out to their advantage. We did turn the ball over and that's what happens.

"The one thing I was happy with is that we didn't give up. We hung in there and nearly pulled out the win."

EVEN IN DEFEAT ISAAC ADDS TO HIS TOTALS

Team	Receptions	Yards	Touchdowns
Baltimore	8	92	1
Atlanta	3	68	1
Cincinnati	6	152	0
San Francisco	5	134	4
Atlanta	6	48	1
Cleveland	4	44	1
Tennessee	6	53	1
SEASON TOTAL	38	591	9

Won 6   Lost 1

Game Eight

The Rams quickly got off on the right foot when their linebacker London Fletcher tackled Lions' running back Greg Hill in the end zone for a safety. The Rams put an early two points on the board.

Rams 2, Lions 0

On the second play of the second quarter starting quarterback Charlie Batch threw a four-yard touchdown pass to WR Germane Crowell to move the Lions out front. The Rams didn't like being behind, and made plans to turn the game around.

Rams 2, Lions 7

With 11:32 remaining in the first half, Ram quarterback Kurt Warner marched his troops eighty-one yards on six plays, finishing with a six-yard scoring strike to tight end Jeff Robinson to give St. Louis the lead for the time being.

Rams 9, Lions 7

Detroit, behind the strong leg of kicker Jason Hanson, again went up by one point when he put a twenty-nine-yarder through the uprights.

Rams 9, Lions 10

Now it was the Rams' turn to go the field goal route as Jeff Wilkins booted one from thirty-four yards out with just forty-one seconds left on the clock giving the Rams the lead once more.

Rams 12, Lions 10

Batch was at quarterback to start the second half but was replaced after just one series because of a hand injury. Gus Frerotte came in and did an outstanding job.

The third quarter had barely gotten underway when Lion cornerback Terry Fair intercepted a Kurt Warner pass and returned it to the St. Louis twelve-yard line. That set up the next score as Frerotte found FB Cory Schlesinger for a three-yard touchdown. The Lions chose to go for the two-point conversion and the Detroit quarterback hit Crowell for the two points.

Rams 12, Lions 18

When Hanson kicked his second field goal of the day, a boot of forty-three yards, it increased their lead to nine points. Time was still not a factor.

Rams 12, Lions 21

As the third quarter was winding down Warner hit wide receiver Az-zahir Hakim with a seventy-five-yard touchdown bomb that excited the whole Rams squad.

Rams 19, Lions 21

Late in the fourth quarter kicker Hanson increased the Detroit lead with a forty-four-yard boot. This was his third field goal of the afternoon.

Rams 19, Lions 24

Not to be outdone, the Rams, facing a fast moving clock, moved down the field behind Warner on an eight-play, eighty-seven-yard drive that culminated in a two-yard touchdown pass to tackle Ryan Tucker who lined up as an eligible receiver to give the Rams the go-ahead points with just 2:42 left in the game. The Rams, too, opted for the two-point conversion and Warner hit Isaac for the two points.

Rams 27, Lions 24

There was only 1:17 left in the contest when on fourth down and twenty-six yards to go for the first down, Frerotte found Crowell open for a 57-yard gain and the first down. Three plays later Frerotte hit Morton in the end zone for the final touchdown.

Final Score: Rams 27, Lions 31

The Rams had now dropped two in a row and the media was playing the tune that St. Louis hadn't played any tough teams and they had a weak schedule and might have a difficult time returning to what they were in the first six games.

Isaac's Comments

"This was the first time I've been around a team that just felt sick with this loss. Ordinarily, the Rams teams that I had played for, we wouldn't have cared that much, we'd just prepare for the next game. But with these guys we're still upset about losing to Tennessee. You know we almost came back against the Lions. They had a fourth down and twenty-six yards for a first down, and Frerotte completed something like a fifty-seven-yard pass."

EVEN AFTER TWO LOSSES ISAAC MOVES AHEAD

Team	Receptions	Yards	Touchdowns
Baltimore	8	92	1
Atlanta	3	68	1
Cincinnati	6	152	0
San Francisco	5	134	4
Atlanta	6	48	1
Cleveland	4	44	1
Tennessee	6	53	1
Detroit	2	34	0 [2-point]
Season Total	38	591	9

Won 6   Lost 2

CHAPTER TWELVE

The Second Half

Game Nine

IT WAS THE MIDWAY POINT OF THE SEASON WHEN THE CAROLINA PANTHERS CAME TO THE TRANS WORLD DOME ON November 14. The Rams were hoping to break a two-game losing streak and get back in the win column. They were a bit concerned when the Panthers took the kickoff and drove downfield with great ease. Panthers QB Steve Beuerlein completed a fourteen-yard touchdown pass in the end zone to big tight end Wesley Walls to give them a seven-point lead. Walls was becoming a Carolina fan favorite.

Rams 0, Panthers 7

But enough was enough, and the Rams took the kickoff and marched down the field for eighty yards on four plays capping the drive with a twenty-two-yard toss to Isaac from Warner. This was Isaac's tenth touchdown pass of the season making him number one in the NFC in TD passes and second in the NFL behind Marvin Harrison of the Indianapolis Colts.

Rams 7, Panthers 7

With fifteen seconds left in the first quarter, the Ram veteran from Notre Dame, CB Todd Lyght, intercepted a Beuerlein pass and returned it fifty-seven yards for another score.

Rams 14, Panthers 7

St. Louis added to their lead when Warner found TE Roland Williams with a nineteen-yard touchdown strike. Williams was becoming another outstanding threat for the Rams, as if trying to cover Bruce, Holt, and Hakim wasn't enough! Kurt Warner, at 6'2" and 220 pounds was built to be an NFL quarterback and would not squander this chance of a lifetime. Against Carolina he threw the ball twenty-nine times, connected on nineteen of them and in doing so used nine different receivers. He moved the Rams down the field on scoring drives of eighty, eighty, and seventy-eight yards. He led the NFL in touchdown passes (twenty-six), completion percentage (68.5), and a quarterback rating of 117.8

Rams 21, Panthers 7

With forty-four seconds remaining in the first half, Carolina placekicker John Kasay put a twenty-four-yarder through the goalposts.

Rams 21, Panthers 10

The Rams' defense was having a big day. Linebacker Mike Jones stripped the ball from TE Walls and raced into the end zone from thirty-seven yards out to score.

Rams 28, Panthers 10

Marshall Faulk capped a good day's work with a twenty-two-yard scamper for a touchdown.

Final Score: Rams 35, Panthers 10

Isaac's Comments

"I ran a post pattern for the twenty-two-yard touchdown pass that Kurt threw." When asked which was his favorite pattern to run he said, "I like them all. I just want to get the ball."

ISAAC CONTINUES TO BUILD ON HIS SEASON RECORD

Team	Receptions	Yards	Touchdowns
Baltimore	8	92	1
Atlanta	3	68	1
Cincinnati	6	152	0
San Francisco	5	134	4
Atlanta	6	48	1
Cleveland	4	44	1
Tennessee	6	53	1
Detroit	2	34	0 [2-point]
Carolina	5	69	1
SEASON TOTAL	43	660	10

Won 7   Lost 2

Game number ten would see St. Louis head to the west coast to take on the San Francisco 49ers at 3Com Park on November 21, their second meeting of the season. It was sunny, but that could be deceiving as the temperature at game time was a chilly fifty-five degrees with the wind blowing off the bay as usual.

The 68,193 fans on hand for this long-running rivalry were hoping their beloved 49ers could rebound and get back to playing winning football. They were not used to seeing their team flounder. Unfortunately for San Francisco this was not to be that day as they went down 23–7 to give the Rams their eighth victory, and a sweep of the season series 2–0. This was the first time since 1980 that the Rams had made that sweep. Another milestone came with the win. This was the first time since moving to St. Louis that they had won eight games.

Game Ten

Rams placekicker Jeff Wilkins got the scoring underway when he booted a forty-yard field goal with 4:47 left in the first quarter.

Rams 3, 49ers 0

Late in the first half San Francisco quarterback, Steve Stenstrom took the Niner's downfield on a sustained drive with RB Fred Beasley going over from the one-yard line for the touchdown.

Rams 3, 49ers 7

But the Rams took the lead for good with their next drive when QB Kurt Warner hit number 80 for a five-yard touchdown. With that scoring catch, Isaac would move into fifth place on the St. Louis career touchdown reception list with forty.

Warner now had completed at least one touchdown pass in each of the Rams' games. He continued to move the ball around hitting six different receivers on 22 of 40 passes for 201 yards. He then led the NFL with 27 touchdown passes. His completion percentage was 66.8, 2649 yards passing, 213 completed passes, and a quarterback rating of 111.4, all tops in the league.

Rams 10, 49ers 7

Wilkens kicked his second field goal of the game on the last play of the first half. The ball went through from twenty yards out.

Rams 13, 49ers 7

Still early in the third quarter DT D'Marco Farr tipped a Steve Stenstrom pass that sailed into the hands of LB Mike Jones who returned it forty-four yards for the touchdown. This was by far one of the best defensive games of the season for the Rams.

Rams 20, 49ers 7

Wilkins finished the scoring for the day when he hit on his third field goal of the day, a forty-nine-yard shot.

Final Score: Rams 23, 49ers 7

Isaac's Comments

"This was the second time we played against the 49ers this season. This time it was at their place, and I think they played much better. Maybe it was the home crowd. Their offense was having most of their problems. They couldn't settle on a quarterback and that always hurts you. We have a great defense too. A lot of fans think the Rams are all offense but our defense is as good as anybody's in the league.

"Fortunately, we were able to adapt to playing on that field that they have there and come out with a victory."

ISAAC'S RECORDS AFTER TEN GAMES

Team	Receptions	Yards	Touchdowns
Baltimore	8	92	1
Atlanta	3	68	1
Cincinnati	6	152	0
San Francisco	5	134	4
Atlanta	6	48	1
Cleveland	4	44	1
Tennessee	6	53	1
Detroit	2	34	0 [2-point]
Carolina	5	69	1
San Francisco	11	93	1
Season Total	54	753	11

Won 8   Lost 2

Game Eleven

Now back on their winning ways, St. Louis posted their first winning season since 1989 against the weary New Orleans Saints in the Trans World Dome on November 28. Kick returner Tony Horne gave the Rams great field position when he took the opening kickoff back for sixty-four yards to the New Orleans thirty-yard line. Three plays later QB Kurt Warner found Torry Holt open for a 25-yard touchdown strike.

Rams 7, Saints 0

Saints kicker Doug Brien kicked his first of four field goals for the game when he put one through from fifty-one yards.

Rams 7, Saints 3

On the first play of the second quarter Brien connected again this time with a forty-two-yarder to bring the Saints closer.

Rams 7, Saints 6

Brien was fast becoming the entire offense for New Orleans hitting his third field goal try in as many attempts and putting the Saints out in front.

Rams 7, Saints 9

Horne again made a sensational kickoff return bringing the ball back for forty-one yards. Isaac was giving the Saints secondary fits when cornerback Ashley Ambrose interfered with him causing a thirty-five-yard interference penalty. This put the ball on the New Orleans fourteen-yard line. Just five plays later RB Marshall Faulk ran the ball in from the one-yard line. Then he finished the drive running in a two-point conversion. He collected 102 yards on eighteen carries to gather his fifth one hundred-yard rushing game of the year. At this point he was sixth in the NFL in rushing with 908 yards.

Rams 15, Saints 9

Brien, still trying to keep the Saints close, kicked his fourth field goal of the day hoping to cut the Rams' lead at halftime. But he couldn't do it by himself.

Rams 15, Saints 12

The New Orleans kicker proved he wasn't Superman when on the first drive of the second half he could have tied the game for the Saints but his kick hit the left goal-post.

On the ensuing drive following the kickoff, the Rams moved down the field with Marshall Faulk scoring his second touchdown of the day with a six-yard run. He ranked fourth in the NFC in total yards from scrimmage.

Rams 22, Saints 12

Robert Holcombe, the Rams running back, finished a seven play, sixty-seven-yard drive when he scored on a three-yard run with 12:15 left in the game.

Rams 29, Saints 12

Next it was Kurt Warner connecting with Torry Holt on a twenty-yard touchdown pass. It was Holt's second of the day. Completing fifteen of twenty-seven passes to five different receivers, Kurt was the leader in the NFC and third in the NFL in total passing yards with 2,862. At the time, Peyton Manning with 2,952 and Drew Bledsoe with 2,890 were the only players that were ahead of him in the NFL.

Rams 36, Saints 12

Scoring his first ever NFL touchdown, rookie RB James Hodgins out of San Jose State finished out the scoring for the Rams with a one-yard run. Hodgins also had a very good day on special teams making two tackles. This final drive was quarterbacked by Paul Justin, the five-year backup out of Arizona State.

Even though Isaac didn't actually score a touchdown, he still accounted for a pretty big chunk of the Rams' offense. Isaac had five receptions for eighty-one yards which included the game's longest—thirty-three yards. He was then tied with Cris Carter of the Minnesota Vikings in touchdown receptions with eleven.

Final Score: Rams 43, Saints 12

Isaac's Comments

"It was just too bad for the Saints—they just didn't have enough quality players. Not saying anything derogatory, but they just didn't have the players on defense to make the plays. You've got to remember we had a very big arsenal of offensive and defensive weapons and we used them well."

ISAAC BRUCE

ISAAC'S NUMBERS GROW

Team	Receptions	Yards	Touchdowns
Baltimore	8	92	1
Atlanta	3	68	1
Cincinnati	6	152	0
San Francisco	5	134	4
Atlanta	6	48	1
Cleveland	4	44	1
Tennessee	6	53	1
Detroit	2	34	0 [2-point]
Carolina	5	69	1
San Francisco	11	93	1
New Orleans	5	81	0
SEASON TOTAL	59	834	11

Won 9   Lost 2

CHAPTER THIRTEEN

Rams Clinch Playoff Berth

IN GAME NUMBER TWELVE OF THE SEASON, THE RAMS CLINCHED A PLAYOFF BERTH FOR THE FIRST TIME SINCE 1989. THE CAROLINA PANTHERS fell before them 34–21. This also gave them the division title, and that hadn't been done since 1985.

This was one of the best team efforts in every area of the game. Isaac pulled in six passes for 111 yards. He recorded his twenty-first career one hundred-yard game and moved into a tie for second with Elroy "Crazy Legs" Hirsch. He was sixth in the NFL with 67 receptions.

Game Twelve

Kurt Warner continued his magic touch when he drove the Rams down the field sixty-nine yards on nine plays and found TE Roland Williams for a fourteen-yard touchdown. The big tight end had caught five touchdown passes—an all-time high for him.

Rams 7, Panthers 0

There was 5:14 to go in the first quarter when Warner threw his second touchdown pass of the day, this time he hit Az-zahir Hakim with a forty-eight-yard bomb. Hakim had a career day, gaining 122 yards through the air. He was also ranked number five in the NFL in average punt returns with 12.0.

Rams 14, Panthers 0

St. Louis took a commanding lead when Warner hit Hakim again for another forty-nine-yard touchdown pass. Warner now had thrown three touchdown passes in eight of the Rams' games. He led the NFL in about every category that a quarterback competes in. His rating was an unbelievable 142.3.

Rams 21, Panthers 0

As the clock was running down, there were only forty-one seconds left in the first half and Carolina got on the board when Panther QB Steve Beuerlein found TE Wesley Walls for a fifteen-yard touchdown pass making the halftime score 21–7.

Rams 21, Panthers 7

The Carolina quarterback completed his second scoring pass to WR Donald Hayes with a thirty-six-yard toss. Even in a losing effort Beuerlein had an outstanding game.

Rams 21, Panthers 14

On the first play of the fourth quarter Rams kicker Jeff Wilkins hit on a forty-four-yard boomer. This moved him into third place on the Rams' career list of highest field goal percentage, surpassing Mike Lansford with a 72.8 percent.

Rams 24, Panthers 14

Beuerlein, the Panther quarterback, hit on his third touchdown pass of the afternoon when he found WR Patrick Jeffers, who went seventy-one yards for the score.

Rams 24, Panthers 21

But when Beuerlein went to the well once too often Rams cornerback, Dre' Bly put the game out of reach when he picked off a pass and returned it fifty-three yards for a touchdown. For Bly, a rookie from North Carolina, it was his first NFL touchdown.

Rams 31, Panthers 21

Dependable Jeff Wilkins hit on a forty-four-yard field goal to bring the final score to:

Final Score: Rams 34, Panthers 21

Marshall Faulk got his sixth one hundred-yard game as a Ram. He became the first Ram since Jerome Bettis to rush for at least one thousand yards in a season. Against the Panthers he carried the ball twenty-two times for 118 yards.

Isaac's Comments

"Scoring nearly thirty points a game came as no surprise to us. We knew if Kurt could just get the ball into our hands we could make things happen and we did. We were all happy to be back on the winning ways and we really didn't want to entertain another defeat this year."

RAM TEAM RECORDS FALL FOR ISAAC

Team	Receptions	Yards	Touchdowns
Baltimore	8	92	1
Atlanta	3	68	1
Cincinnati	6	152	0
San Francisco	5	134	4
Atlanta	6	48	1
Cleveland	4	44	1
Tennessee	6	53	1
Detroit	2	34	0 (2-point)
Carolina	5	69	1
San Francisco	11	93	1
New Orleans	5	81	0
Carolina	6	111	0
Season Total	65	945	11

Won 10   Lost 2

All sorts of good things were happening for the Rams. They became the first team in NFL history to post a perfect record in their division with an 8–0 mark—one season after going winless in the division! What a difference a year makes, not to mention a healthy Isaac Bruce and a Marshall Faulk.

Game Thirteen

The Rams came into the Superdome on December 12 to go up against the banged-up Saints. New Orleans got the ball and drove down close to the Rams' goal line, where placekicker Doug Brien drilled a 29-yard field goal to give the Saints a short-lived lead.

Rams 0, Saints 3

After driving the ball down the field fifty-nine yards on nine plays, Kurt Warner capped it off with a scoring toss of one yard to RB Robert Holcombe, the first of his career.

Rams 7, Saints 3

It was time for the Saints kicker, Brien, to try another field goal this time from 26-yards out. The kick was perfect.

Rams 7, Saints 6

With Billy Joe Tolliver at quarterback for New Orleans, the Saints immediately scored with a two-yard touchdown pass to TE Cameron Cleveland. Tolliver hit WR Eddie Kennison for the two-point conversion.

Rams 7, Saints 14

From that point on the game was all St. Louis. Wilkins hit another forty-yard field goal to put the Rams in striking position.

Rams 10, Saints 14

On the Saints next possession, CB Todd Lyght picked off a Tolliver pass and returned it twenty-two yards to the

St. Louis forty-one-yard line. That set up a six play fifty-nine-yard drive that resulted in Marshall Faulk going over from the four-yard line. Faulk continued his MVP season when he rushed for more than one hundred yards for the fourth consecutive week. He posted 154 yards on 29 carries, while pulling in five receptions for 56 yards. He then led the NFL with a 5.3 yards per-carry average. (For rushers who have gained one thousand yards or more.) He was truly an iron man.

Rams 17, Saints 14

Rams CB Dexter McCleon intercepted another Tolliver pass and gave the Rams great field position. On the next series of downs Warner completed a thirty-yard touchdown pass to the fleet Faulk.

Warner continued to rack up records like they were nothing. At this point of the season he was leading the NFL quarterbacks in all statistical categories. He moved into fourth place on the Rams' list of single season passing yards, surpassing Jim Everett (1991).

Rams 24, Saints 14

The Rams' kicker, Wilkins, hit two more field goals, bringing his total for the day to three, booting them from thirty yards and thirty-eight yards to finish off the scoring.

Final Score: Rams 30, Saints 14

Isaac finished the day with another one hundred-yard plus day on four catches. He moved into sole possession of second on the Rams' all-time list of one hundred-yard receiving games. Gathering the 102 yards gave him his third one thousand-yard receiving season in his six-year career.

Isaac's Comments

"When we went up against the Saints this second time we expected about the same as the first game and that's what we got. Fortunately, I was able to get several big gainers. They just can't cover all of us. Someone's always open or Marshall is running crazy."

ISAAC'S GAME 13 TOTALS

Team	Receptions	Yards	Touchdowns
Baltimore	8	92	1
Atlanta	3	68	1
Cincinnati	6	152	0
San Francisco	5	134	4
Atlanta	6	48	1
Cleveland	4	44	1
Tennessee	6	53	1
Detroit	2	34	0 [2-point]
Carolina	5	69	1
San Francisco	11	93	1
New Orleans	5	81	0
Carolina	6	111	0
New Orleans	4	102	0
Season Total	69	1047	11

Won 11   Lost 2

CHAPTER FOURTEEN

Home Field Advantage

Game Fourteen

THE RAMS WERE BACK IN THE FRIENDLY CONFINES OF THE TRANS WORLD DOME FOR THE FOURTEENTH GAME OF the season against the fast charging New York Giants. St. Louis had clinched a first-round bye and home-field advantage throughout the playoffs when they won their record-tying twelfth game of the season. The Giants could pose a threat to the Rams who had vowed not to loose another game this season.

A dome record crowd of 66,665 football fans were on hand, and excitement was in the air as their team looked almost unbeatable. But as they say, "on any given Sunday . . ."

Jeff Wilkins, the St. Louis kicker, started off the scoring with a booming forty-seven-yard field goal putting the Rams up 3–0.

Rams 3, Giants 0

After New York couldn't sustain a drive they punted the ball, and with 13:31 left in the first half Kurt Warner found Az-zahir Hakim at the back of the zone for a three-yard touchdown. He was pushed out of bounds as he made the catch. His three receptions were good for seventy-nine yards and two touchdowns

Rams 10, Giants 0

Taking the kickoff, the Giants moved downfield to get into position for placekicker Cory Blanchard to put one through the uprights from twenty-three yards out and get New York on the scoreboard.

Rams 10, Giants 3

The St. Louis defense got into the scoring act when free safety Devin Bush, the five-year player out of Florida State, intercepted Kerry Collins, the New York quarterback and raced forty-five yards to score. This was Bush's first career touchdown.

Rams 17, Giants 3

Again the Rams' defense held the Giants, forcing them to punt again. Warner went right back to work hitting Hakim on a short pass that the flying wide receiver caught and then broke a number of tackles en route to a sixty-five-yard score. This was Warner's second TD pass of the day. He completed eighteen of thirty-two for 319 yards . . . moved into a tie for fifth place on the NFL's list of single season touchdown passes with thirty-six, tying George Blanda, Y. A. Tittle, and Steve Young. He passed for three hundred yards for the eighth time that year, tying Dan Fouts of the San Diego Chargers.

Rams 24, Giants 3

It was a defensive day. With only 7:10 left in the game, the Rams' defense was fired up when LB Mike Jones, the veteran from the University of Missouri, picked off a Collins pass and went the distance for a twenty-two-yard touchdown.

Rams 31, Giants 3

Fighting until the end, the Giant QB Collins threw a seven-yard touchdown pass to wide receiver Ike Hilliard. But it was a case of 'too little, too late.'

Isaac finished the day with thirty-nine yards on just two receptions. He was then seventh in the NFL in receptions with seventy-three. He ranked ninth in the NFL in receiving yards with 1120. His 68 points was second, behind Cris Carter on the Minnesota Vikings. Marshall Faulk led all Rams rushers with sixty-eight yards on sixteen tries . . . now third in the NFL in rushing with 1,248 yards, behind Davis of the Washington Redskins (1,405) and James of the Indianapolis Colts (1,400).

Final Score: Rams 31, Giants 10

Isaac's Comments

"The Giants game was a big one for us. We all wanted that one in a big way because the sportswriters were saying that we hadn't played anyone tough yet and the Giants were fighting for a playoff spot. We knew it was going to be a good game. For them it was like a playoff game. They had to win or watch the playoffs on TV. I got a lot of double coverage that game. But it was a team effort."

ISAAC'S STATISTICS INCREASE

Team	Receptions	Yards	Touchdowns
Baltimore	8	92	1
Atlanta	3	68	1
Cincinnati	6	152	0
San Francisco	5	134	4
Atlanta	6	48	1
Cleveland	4	44	1
Tennessee	6	53	1
Detroit	2	34	0 (2-point)
Carolina	5	69	1
San Francisco	11	93	1
New Orleans	5	81	0
Carolina	6	111	0
New Orleans	4	102	0
New York	2	39	0
SEASON TOTAL	71	1086	11

Won 12   Lost 2

Game Fifteen

Looking to have a perfect 8–0 record at home, St. Louis would entertain the Chicago Bears at the Trans World Dome on the day after Christmas. Another record crowd of 65,941 filled the stadium and got to see the Rams win their eighth home game of the season to bring Christmas joy to their fans.

A scoreless first quarter had the teams exchanging punts. The Rams struck first when Kurt Warner found Marshall Faulk on a screen pass and the running back did his thing, breaking tackles, making tacklers miss and outrunning them into the end zone to cap a forty-eight-yard gain. Faulk added to his already hefty record as he became only the second player in NFL history to both rush and receive one thousand yards in a season. Roger Craig of the San Francisco 49ers was the other. They both have the same kind of work ethic.

Rams 7, Bears 0

Chicago couldn't put any offense together so it was out in three, punt, out in three, punt. That pattern was killing them, because St. Louis easily scored on its next four possessions. The Rams' strong safety Billy Jenkins then intercepted a pass from the Bears' rookie quarterback Cade McNown to stop a Chicago drive and set up the next Rams score. Jenkins was everywhere on defense. He had ten tackles, nine of them solos, and the interception.

For their second score the Rams moved down the field on a seven-play, eighty-three-yard touchdown drive, with Kurt Warner hitting TE Roland Williams for the score. This would be one of three drives of eighty yards or more on which the rookie quarterback would direct his team. He now led the NFL, and was tied with Dan Marino (1984 Dolphins) and Warren Moon (1990 Oilers) with nine three hundred-yard passing games in a regular season.

Rams 14, Bears 0

There were only forty-eight seconds left in the first half when Rams kicker Jeff Wilkins kicked a thirty-eight-yard field goal to extend the St. Louis lead.

Rams 17, Bears 0

Next, Warner connected with Isaac on a four-yard touchdown pass. This was Warner's third TD pass of the game. Isaac had four receptions for forty-five yards. He rushed for eleven yards on two carries.

Rams 24, Bears 0

When Rams defensive end Grant Wistrom picked off a Shane Matthews pass and returned it forty yards for the score, he became the team record holder with eight defensive touchdowns.

Rams 31, Bears 0

Chicago finally scored its first touchdown with three minutes to go in the third quarter when Matthews threw an eight-yard pass to WR Bobby Engram.

Rams 31, Bears 6

Matthews again found Engram on their next possession with a four-yard scoring pass. Engram ended the day with 143 yards on thirteen catches. Not bad in a losing cause.

Rams 31, Bears 12

Jeff Wilkins finished the scoring when he kicked a twenty-eight-yard field goal.

Final Score: Rams 34, Bears 12

Isaac's Comments

"Playing the Bears is a lot like playing San Francisco, it's always a big rivalry. They've always been spoilers, and nothing would make their season like beating the Rams. We were ready to play. They weren't going to catch us sleeping or looking beyond them."

ONE MORE TO GO FOR ISAAC

Team	Receptions	Yards	Touchdowns
Baltimore	8	92	1
Atlanta	3	68	1
Cincinnati	6	152	0
San Francisco	5	134	4
Atlanta	6	48	1
Cleveland	4	44	1
Tennessee	6	53	1
Detroit	2	34	0 [2-point]
Carolina	5	69	1
San Francisco	11	93	1
New Orleans	5	81	0
Carolina	6	111	0
New Orleans	4	102	0
New York	2	39	0
Chicago	4	45	1
SEASON TOTAL	75	1131	11

Won 13   Lost 2

Game Sixteen

When the St. Louis team went to Veterans Stadium on January 2 to meet the Philadelphia Eagles, for all intents and purposes the game didn't mean much to the Rams. They had already gained the home field advantage throughout the playoffs and they would use this game to give some of the younger players a shot to play and to rest the veterans. Isaac only played in the first series and then watched from the sideline as the Eagles won the game 38–31.

Marshall Faulk caught an eight-yard shovel pass from Kurt Warner on his way to breaking the NFL's all-time record of 2,358 yards from scrimmage in a single season. (The record was previously held by the now retired Barry Sanders of the Detroit Lions, 1997.) He finished the game with 2,429 yards.

Even in a losing effort and only playing the first half Warner continued to set or tie new passing records. His two touchdown passes of the day gave him a season high of forty-one. Only Dan Marino of the Dolphins had done better throwing forty-eight in 1983 and then forty-four in 1986.

Rams 7, Eagles 0

After receiving the kickoff the 'Iggles' got into field goal range to allow kicker David Akers to put one through from 46 yards out.

Rams 7, Eagles 3

Following an eight-play drive good for eighty-six yards, Faulk then ran it in from the one-yard line for the score.

Rams 14, Eagles 3

Taking the kickoff and moving the ball ahead gave Philadelphia a boost, and then the Eagle quarterback, Donovan McNabb, hit WR Torrence Small with a sixty-three-yard pass and a touchdown.

Rams 14, Eagles 10

With a little more than six minutes left in the first half Jeff Wilkins booted a forty-seven-yard field goal to extend the Rams' lead.

Rams 17, Eagles 10

But Philly wasn't down yet. McNabb completed his second touchdown pass of the day when he got the ball to RB Duce Staley on a shovel pass. He carried it in from the three-yard line with just twenty-five seconds to go in the first half.

Rams 17, Eagles 17

A fired up Eagles team took the field for the second half with victory in their nostrils. They had played the powerful Rams to a tie in the first half and planned to do even better in the second half.

The Rams took the opening kickoff, but disaster struck on their first drive when Eagles DE Mike Mamula picked off a Warner pass and returned it forty-one yards to put Philadelphia on top.

Rams 17, Eagles 24

Warner brought the Rams back, going sixty-seven yards on six plays and finishing with a fifteen-yard pass to Torry Holt to tie the game. That would end the action for the day for Warner.

Rams 24, Eagles 24

With 10:55 to play in the game McNabb completed a five-yard pass to TE Chad Lewis and a touchdown to return the lead to the Eagles.

Rams 24, Eagles 31

Joe Germaine, another rookie quarterback out of Ohio State, replaced Warner for St. Louis, and this would be the first time he would see extensive playing time. He made good use of his time as he completed nine of sixteen passes for 136 yards and the first two touchdowns of his NFL career. He also threw the longest pass of his career, a sixty-three-yard bomb to Torry Holt.

The young quarterback got of to a bad start though when Eagles CB Al Harris returned an interception for seventeen yards and the score.

Rams 31, Eagles 38

The Rams went for the onside kick, but Philadelphia fell on the ball, and from there McNabb took three quick knees and the Eagle victory.

Final Score: Rams 31, Eagles 38

Isaac's Comments

"We would have liked to win the game, of course but we didn't have anything to prove. The playoffs were here and that's what was important to us at that time. I feel if we had needed to beat the Eagles to get into the playoffs it would have been a different game with a different outcome."

ISAAC'S AMAZING TOTALS

Team	Receptions	Yards	Touchdowns
Baltimore	8	92	1
Atlanta	3	68	1
Cincinnati	6	152	0
San Francisco	5	134	4
Atlanta	6	48	1
Cleveland	4	44	1
Tennessee	6	53	1
Detroit	2	34	0 [2-point]
Carolina	5	69	1
San Francisco	11	93	1
New Orleans	5	81	0
Carolina	6	111	0
New Orleans	4	102	0
New York	2	39	0
Chicago	4	45	1
Philadelphia	0	0	0

Won 13   Lost 3

ISAAC BRUCE

Season Totals

Games Started/Games Played	16/16
Receptions	77
Total Receiving Yards	1,165
Average Yardage Per Reception	15.1
Longest Reception	60
Touchdowns	12
Rushing Plays	5
Total Rushing Yards	32
Average Yards Per Rushing Play	6.4
Longest Rushing Play	11
Rushing Touchdowns	0

The St. Louis Rams were the National Football Conference Champions!

CHAPTER FIFTEEN

Super Bowl Week

THE RAMS CAME THROUGH THE NFC PLAYOFFS WITH NO MAJOR INJURIES AND WITH HIGH HOPES OF REVENGE ON THE TENNESSEE Titans who had beaten St. Louis in a close game in Nashville a few weeks earlier. In that game the Titans got out in front in a hurry, scoring twenty-one points in the first quarter. This was one thing the Rams did not want to let happen in Super Bowl XXXIV.

The Rams placekicker, Jeff Wilkins, was still hampered by an injury to his plant leg but insisted it would be okay by game time.

There would only be one week between the last playoff game and the Super Bowl. Both head coaches said they liked the two week layoff best but had to live with this format. The game would be played with only one week of preparation.

The St. Louis squad arrived by charter in Atlanta on Monday afternoon but had no scheduled practices until Wednesday. Rams Head Coach Dick Vermeil and his coaching staff remained in St. Louis to prepare the big game plan. They would arrive late Tuesday ready to implement the way to turn the tide on the Titans. This would be Vermeil's second Super Bowl appearance. The first was in Super Bowl XV, in which the Philadelphia Eagles lost to the Oakland Raiders 27–10. He had learned from that game not to get his guys wound too tight. At sixty-three years old, if he could get the victory he could become the oldest head coach to win a Super Bowl. He scheduled no curfews for the week. All the practices were closed to the public and the media and were heavily guarded. The way his team had responded to his hyper personality was amazing, and now they are ready to win one for the Coach.

If you were planning on coming to the Super Bowl and you were not yet hooked up with lodging, you were in big trouble because it was announced that there were no rooms available within a fifty-mile radius. You had to take a sleeping bag.

The Bruce clan at the super Bowl in Atlanta.

154

Anna and Christy eating breakfast in hotel before a game.

After checking into the Crowne Plaza Ravinia Hotel in Dunwoody, the Rams players took some time to take care of all the little, sometimes annoying, things that go with being part of Super Bowl week. Ticket requests always send players and coaches scurrying to fill their needs. Each player is allocated thirteen tickets they can purchase and two comps. That's it. Fifteen tickets and fifty requests. The earlier they could get it done the more they could focus on the job at hand.

Everyone was trying a few restaurants like Justin's, or Mako's, a popular place for the ballplayers, not only those playing in the big game but other NFL stars who were in town to see the big show.

Tuesday and Wednesday were media days. The NFL set up tents in the hotel parking lots and the sessions were mandatory for players and coaches. This is probably, next to the game itself, the hardest part of the week for the players and coaches to endure. The same questions are asked over and over again and the players answer each time like it was the first time it was asked. The clichés would be nonstop. This would be the most covered sporting event in the world. Among the foreign countries' media present were Mexico, Japan, and Germany.

Wednesday the freezing weather didn't help the scribes, who were turning blue from the cold and were having trouble getting their questions out. You could see the players' breath as they fielded questions from the blue-lipped journalists. On Thursday the NFL brought in a few more heaters to warm things up. The weather forecast didn't sound good—snow tonight and cold throughout the weekend.

In his article "Dumb Questions," Vic Carucci of *NFL Insider* magazine listed his favorites from past Super Bowls:

To Patriots guard Heath Irwin, before Super Bowl XXXI: "Would you like to win the AFC with the Super Bowl?"

To Redskins QB Doug Williams, before Super Bowl XXX: "How long have you been a black quarterback?" (This has since been uncovered as a myth.)

To long-locked Steelers linebacker Kevin Greene, before Super Bowl XXXIII: "How long does it take you to wash your hair?" Go figure!

To Broncos QB John Elway, before Super Bowl XXIX: "Are you going to listen to Stevie Wonder perform at half-time?"

To 49ers guard Ralph Tamm, before Super Bowl XXIX: "Is Steve Young really a good player?"

The questions offered up by the media at Super Bowl XXXIV were not much better. There were a few like: To

Karetha Bruce and her friend Shawn relaxing before the big game.

Isaac Bruce, "Are you as fast as you look?" To Kurt Warner, "Does it hurt when you're blindsided by a blitzing linebacker?" To Marshall Faulk, "Do you think St. Louis has a chance to win this time?"

But most of the players, especially the young players and those that do not play positions that get their name in print, have a lot of fun with the sportswriters. There are many writers and broadcasters from small markets, and this game was an event of a lifetime for them.

It was bantered about all week by the media what a loss it was that the teams that were playing in the NFL's biggest show were from relatively small markets. Could these two teams, or the MVP quarterback with his speed burning receivers, hold an audience's attention for nearly four hours?

The game would be played inside the state-owned Georgia Dome located in downtown Atlanta. It is the

Top: Rosalind and Charlotte Bruce at Adelphia Coliseum in Nashville, Tennessee.

Bottom: Karetha Bruce with her sister Sarah and brother John in Elmira, New York.

Left: Christina at breakfast the morning of the Super Bowl.

Below: Jonathan and Caleb, two of Isaac's nephews.

Rosalind eating breakfast on Super Bowl Sunday.

largest cable-supported domed stadium in the world. The Rams players said they thought the Georgia Dome field was a little bit harder than the Trans World Dome field.

Wednesday's practice was much like any other first practice of the week with the exception of the freezing cold. The Rams practiced at the Atlanta Falcons outdoor facility and finding a way to keep warm was the toughest thing. The heaters that were brought to the field were of little help.

The Rams were loose in practice and looked to be confident and ready to play. The last thing they wanted was to be uptight and play into the Titans' hands.

Thursday was a day for the players to try to shake off the pain from the practice the day before. Again it was a time to answer questions from the media—who seemed to be everywhere. The day's practice went as planned for the Rams as they continued to fine tune their game plan. Some of the players were already feeling the butterflies in their stomachs, but to others it was just another day at the office.

Family members and friends started to pour into Atlanta, some coming a day early trying to beat a new storm front that was moving into the area. It would be the last night the team members would have to go out with their people.

Friday would see the Rams practicing inside in the Georgia Dome. This was Isaac Bruce's favorite stadium in which to play. He had had a great deal of success here and he wouldn't be disappointed come Sunday!

Coming into the stadium for practice, the players were a bit overwhelmed when they saw the red, white, and blue bunting all around the bleachers, the NFL logo at midfield, and the team's name in the end zone.

Family, Faith, and the Final Touchdown

The team didn't wear pads for the practice. In fact it had been seven weeks since the Rams last practiced with full gear. The Titans were just finishing their indoor practice, and now it was the Rams' turn. They went over all aspects of the game, zeroing in on special teams. Frank Gansz, the special teams coach, known as "Crash," demonstrated his genius to pay attention to every detail no matter how small it might seem! The men on the special teams knew they could have a chance to win or loose a game depending on their play. The special teams players would only be in the game for a few plays but those plays could and would determine the outcome of the game.

One of the main reasons for practicing in the dome was to get used to the lights. Every stadium's lights are a little different. You must get accustomed to the trajectory of the ball and the way a receiver sees it coming.

It was a day for Rams part owner, Stan Kroenke, to speak to the team. He's a man that the players respect. He and majority owner Georgia Frontiere would be there to support their team. The Rams and their owners wouldn't be watching the Super Bowl on television. Now it was their turn to experience the wonderful feeling of winning the NFC championship and going to the Super Bowl.

Saturday was a light day just going over assignments and running through the game plan.

Finally Sunday arrived, and the weather in Atlanta was the best it had been all week. Now it was time for the biggest game of the season for some one hundred players and coaches.

The stadium was filled with thousands of screaming, hollering fans. The contingency from St. Louis was there for their first time Super Bowl as "Rams" as were the Tennessee Titans.

Bruce family members show their Rams pride. Pictured are: Anna, Sylvia, Karetha, Rosalind, Isaac, Johnathan, Christina, and family friend Shawn.

All week the comparisons between the Rams rookie quarterback, Kurt Warner out of Northern Iowa, and Titans QB Steve McNair from Alcorn State, kept the reporters' computers busy. Warner, named NFL MVP had a season that was right out of a fiction adventure book. It might even be a best-seller. McNair was coming off his best season and was healthy following an injury in game one. He missed five games but came back to have a breakout year. He was as big a threat to run the ball as he was to throw it. Somehow he always seemed to escape trouble that would have meant a sack to other quarterbacks.

The coaches were ready and chomping at the bit. The players wanted to get the game started. The fans in the stadium, watching on television, and listening on radios were set. Now the slowest clock in the world would start turning until it was 3:00 P.M. and Super Bowl XXXIV would be underway.

CHAPTER SIXTEEN

The Game

IT ALL COMES DOWN TO SIXTY MINUTES OF FOOTBALL PLAYED BY THE REPRESENTATIVE CHAMPIONS OF THE NFC AND THE AFC. Forty-five players on each team spent eighteen weeks pointing to this one game of football. But this game was like no other. Sure the players would each receive in the neighborhood of $105,000, but that was not what spurred them on. It was the ring! The ring that goes to the winners, who are acclaimed champions of the world.

The happiest man in the world that day was the one who had been in Las Vegas before the season and just because he was a Rams fan laid down one thousand dollars on St. Louis to win the Super Bowl. The fact that it was still July and the preseason had not yet gotten underway made no difference to the loyal fan. It wasn't the 200 to 1 odds that made him make the bet. It was just something to hope for. There was probably some prayer going up for that bet too.

The Titans' strategy was to get in Kurt Warner's face and keep him from getting set to pass. Tennessee had sacked him six times in their previous meeting in the regular season. They ranked third in the NFL with fifty-four sacks. Defensive rookie of the year, Jevon Kearse, was already becoming a premier pass rusher. He had 14.5 sacks in the regular season and two more in the playoffs.

On the other side, the Rams felt they would be able to protect Warner, the league's most valuable player—who had only been sacked twenty-nine times. He went through three games without a sack. And with all the offensive weapons at their disposal they would be able to take care of business.

This would be the first NFL title game for the Rams since 1951 and the first ever for the St. Louis Rams.

The early betting line showed the Rams by a touchdown. A lot of that was due to all the speed they had, along with a rookie quarterback who threw for almost 4,500 yards in the regular season.

 ## The Super Bowl

The Rams took the opening kickoff and moved down to the Titans seventeen-yard line. Twice they made big plays with third and long. But this time they were forced to go for the field goal. PK Jeff Wilkins came in on his gimpy leg. But holder Mike Horan fumbled the snap on what would have been a thirty-five-yard attempt and Tennessee fell on the ball on its own twenty-nine-yard line.

The Titans got to the Rams twenty-six on a screen pass from McNair to Eddie George, a play good for thirty-two yards. After a delay-of-game penalty Al Del Greco missed a forty-seven-yard field goal try.

Warner came back with two quick passes, one to Torry Holt for thirty-two yards and one to Marshall Faulk good for seventeen yards. But the Titans dug in and forced Wilkins to come back in and try a field goal from twenty-seven yards out. This time the kick was good and the Rams took the lead.

Rams 3, Titans 0

Then Warner found Faulk all by himself and the pass was good for fifty-two yards. It took the ball to the seventeen-yard line. But this time Wilkins missed again with only twelve seconds gone from the second quarter.

On the next possession, St. Louis moved the ball down the field seventy-three yards, but the drive stalled at the Tennessee eleven-yard line. This time Wilkins put one through the uprights from twenty-nine yards out.

Rams 6, Titans 0

For the third time in the game the Rams drove to the red zone and seemed to see a stop sign. It was time for Wilkins to kick his third field goal—another twenty-nine-yarder. Even though Warner had yet to throw a touchdown pass he had piled up 277 yards in the first half on nineteen of thirty-five. Warner said, "You can't keep kicking field goals and expect to win." The Rams fleet receivers were wearing down the Titans secondary. Playing in three or four wideout sets on twenty-six of forty-four plays created one-on-one coverage for Isaac Bruce and Torry Holt.

Rams 9, Titans 0

On the opening possession, Tennessee drove to the Rams' twenty-seven-yard line but Del Greco's field goal was blocked by safety Todd Lyght.

St. Louis took the ball from the blocked field goal attempt and put together an eight-play, sixty-eight-yard drive for the game's first touchdown. Torry Holt, the rookie, caught the strike from Warner from the nine-yard line.

Rams 16, Titans 0

The game was halted for twelve minutes when Titans safety Blaine Bishop was treated for what turned out to be a strained neck. The loss of Bishop seemed to ignite Tennessee. The Titans went back to what got them to the Super Bowl in the first place, sending Eddie George inside and getting McNair in position to hit the short passes.

They came back with a sixty-six-yard scoring drive of their own, good for their first score when RB George went in from the one-yard line with fourteen seconds left in the third quarter. The big running back from Ohio State carried seven times on the twelve-play drive. A major part of the drive was a twenty-three-yard scramble to the two-yard line. Going for the two-point conversion, McNair tried to hit TE Frank Wycheck but the ball sailed wide right.

Rams 16, Titans 6

The Titans were not the same team in the second quarter. They were fired up and were taking it to the Rams. St. Louis was forced to punt, and Tennessee wasted no time in getting down the field in thirteen plays, with George carrying eight times, and finishing with a one-yard TD run.

Rams 16, Titans 13

Once again it was three and out for the Rams and Del Greco came in to tie the score with a booming forty-three-yard kick.

Rams 16, Titans 16

But that was when the Rams went to work. The Titans had only tied the game eighteen seconds earlier. But that was long enough for Warner to hit Isaac Bruce on the first down with a pass good for seventy-three yards and the winning touchdown. Isaac made a fantastic adjustment on the ball to beat cornerback Denard Walker. After catching the ball on the Tennessee thirty-nine-yard line he avoided one tackler and raced the other defenders to the goal line. Offensive coordinator Mike Martz decided to go deep to Isaac and see if they could get a quick hit. About the winning call Martz said, "We had five seconds to go before the two-minute warning, and we wanted to take a shot with Isaac over there. I wanted to get the ball into his hands at that point."

Isaac ended the day with six receptions for 162 yards and one touchdown. Warner ended up with 414 yards passing, a new Super Bowl record. "I'm so proud of Kurt," said Isaac. "He had only one week to prepare. Going into the regular season he had only one week to prepare for Baltimore, and look how far he's gone."

Final Score: Rams 23, Titans 16

But the Titans weren't through just yet. A five-yard pass to Kevin Dyson from McNair came within one yard of a potential victory, but Rams linebacker from the University of Missouri, Mike Jones, made a game-saving tackle as Dyson was stretching the ball toward the goal line in vain as the clock ran out. McNair said later, "There were great athletes on both sides of the ball and they made the play. It was a matter of who won the one-on-one battle, and they won."

Forget about the markets being too small or the weather being un-Atlanta like. The fans were treated to what may have been the most exciting Super Bowl ever played and the TV ratings weren't bad either: a 43.0 overnight rating and a 61 share, up 6 percent from last year. With the game going down to the wire, ABC's audience was glued to the screen.

That guy holding the 200 to 1 ticket was one of the happiest men on the planet, but I don't think any member of the St. Louis Rams football team would trade places with him.

Cinderella had come to the ball and danced with the handsome prince!

CHAPTER SEVENTEEN

A Great Year!

IT HAD BEEN A GREAT YEAR FOR THE ST. LOUIS RAMS AND FOR ISAAC BRUCE. ISAAC NOW HAD THE FEELING THAT HE WAS BACK ON TOP OF his game. He had started all sixteen regular season games as well as the playoffs, Super Bowl, and Pro-Bowl. The new training program developed by his coaches and trainers worked as planned. Hard work and determination coupled with his strong belief in Jesus Christ made things happen. That's Isaac Bruce—he makes things happen.

Catching the winning touchdown in the Super Bowl is not just a dream now. It's a reality, and it's something Isaac will be able to tell his grandchildren about in the years to come. And playing on a world championship team—wow! That ring will look good on his finger.

When the Rams returned from Atlanta to St. Louis, fans turned out en masse to welcome their gladiators in an old-fashioned parade featuring the famous Anheiser-Busch Clydesdales and sixty Dodge Ram pickup trucks carrying the players and coaches. The six-block procession was slowed a number of times when energetic fans overpowered a police barrier to get to the champs.

At the ceremony held at Kiener Plaza with the Gateway Arch in the background, head coach Dick Vermeil told the crowd, "As a representative of these guys, the management and the coaching staff, I'd like to thank you for your support. I'd like you to know that the Rams aren't world champions. St. Louis is world champion!" The crowd went wild!

Cardinal red was what most St. Louis fans were used to, but today it was Rams blue and gold.

Things would be different in the year 2000. Dick Vermeil would resign as head coach and Mike Martz would be named head coach.

The off-season following the Super Bowl has kept the young man from Florida busy as you might expect. Unfortunately, he can't go everywhere and do everything he's asked to do because there's just not enough time in the day. He tries to get to those events that benefit people, and where he gets the chance to share his belief in God. His camp at Southern Illinois University in June is a highlight of his off-season.

He'll be sure to get back to Ft. Lauderdale and that wonderful weather, for some of that good soul food his Ma cooks up for him, and I'm sure he'll remind Frank Sanders, Arizona Cardinals wide receiver, how thankful he should be to Isaac for teaching him how to play wide receiver and keeping him off the streets. There won't be any murder ball, but there will be long talks with his brother Lucious. He'll be asked to give his testimony at a number of churches which he will gladly do.

His degree in education will have to wait a spell. He had something important to take care of and couldn't

make the last semester. What was so important you ask? Try the Super Bowl. "Your excused," said his teachers. He'll get his degree next year unless the Rams repeat and that would be okay with Isaac.

He still has time to visit or talk by phone to his old high school and college coaches. He's happy to see Mike Martz move up to the head coaching job with St. Louis. "He'll do just fine," said Isaac.

Every time he picks up a paycheck from the Rams he's thankful he didn't have to earn his way as a roofer. He still wonders how his dad could work so hard in a very difficult job. And his Ma is still his best friend.

Some things change and some don't!

American Sports
Heroes Series

T HE HEART OF AMERICA BEATS WITH A PASSION FOR SPORTS—THE TOIL OF COMPETITION, THE PURSUIT OF EXCELLENCE, the renewed hope that surfaces at the beginning of each new season. So much of this love for sports is due to the athletes themselves. These larger-than-life figures capture our admiration when we are children and our allegiance as we become adults. Week after week we follow them in the sports pages and on radio and television. They are our heroes.

Providence House Publishers has teamed with The Sports Firm, Inc., to develop the AMERICAN SPORTS HEROES SERIES—a collection of sports-themed biographies of popular athletes. These books contain biographical, statistical, and anecdotal information about featured athletes as well as a special section on the athletes' Christian faith and character.